the Texas Provincial Kitchen Cookbook

by Melissa Guerra

The Texas Provincial Kitchen Cookbook

By Melissa Guerra

ISBN 0-9657658-0-6

First Edition

CREDITS:

ART DIRECTION
Lynn Marcantonio

PROOF READING
Roxana Alaniz, Lynn Marcantonio

PHOTOGRAPHY
Cary Whitenton

Assisted by: Dean Jones

FOOD STYLING
Rose Rankin

Assisted by: Kristin Nelson, Betty Lee Wilson, Ali Sosa, Nancy Hawkins

For my husband and children

I love my kitchen table. My husband made it. My kids beat it up. My sneaky brother carved his name in it. I put ladders on it to change light bulbs and clean ceiling fans. Sometimes I knead bread on it. And towards the middle of every day, I clear it off, wipe it down, set it with dishes and a table cloth, and serve our meal.

I guess most kitchen tables are the same as mine. Meals come, meals go, day in, day out. But my family has unwittingly turned this simple piece of wood into a silent observer. If it could talk...goodness, what it would reveal. The biggest, most crucial decisions in our family are discussed here. The hottest, juiciest gossip is repeated on this site. We talk about financial dreams and woes. We get into fights, we kiss and make up. All at this table.

Foreword

And on it, I feed my children. I know what foods they like... I know which ones they'll turn down. There, I place their birthday presents and Valentine's Day candy. I cut out their Halloween costumes, and color their Easter eggs. I nourish their little bodies, and feed their futures with a bounty of nostalgia.

Our kitchen goes beyond meals. It is our shrine, full of rituals and aromas, dedicated to the furtherance of our faith in ourselves. My mother, grandmothers, and their mothers and grandmothers were the keepers of this hearth flame, and now the torch is passed to me and my generation.

Sadly, busy schedules and the microwave oven have stolen much of the aura of the kitchen table. Nobody takes time to sit and have a meal together, much less talk about the going ons of the day. We miss each other terribly. No amount of added salt, fat, sugar, or fancy packaging can take the place of a family gathered together; praying, eating, and simply being a family.

A lot of us have turned our kitchen into museums of the past, it seems. Antique kitchen implements are the rage. It is quite stylish now to seek out those old vinyl and chrome dinettes from the 1950's, as well as the dishes of that era. Everything is retro. Why? Because they bring back the memories of the way kitchens and kitchen tables used to be. The way they ought to be.

Make time to spend time with the people you love. And wipe off that table.

The recipes, food and menus are representative of the cuisine of Texas, more particularly of the Rio Grande Valley, where I was born and raised. Our food in the Valley is like no other. The predominance of Mexican foods and traditions comes from our proximity to the Mexican border. But, as we are still part of the Lone Star State, we have a penchant for Southern foods. The French and Spanish have flown flags over Texas. The flavor of their presence is still alive in our regional dishes. And families from all over the world have settled in Texas, with the hope of finding the right patch of farmland to realize their dreams, looking for the affordable storefront to open their business. Thank goodness that all of them remembered to bring their recipe boxes.

We Texans love to mix the flavors of all our traditions. Our fried chicken and hamburger stands serve jalapeños, *taquitos*, biscuits with gravy, and catfish. I love flour tortillas wrapped around polish sausage. Every Mexican restaurant here serves iced tea, the definitive Southern beverage.

What adds to the authentic presentation of any dish are the side dishes with which it is combined. No food dish is an island. Each depends on other dishes to compliment, contrast, and reveal its flavors. *Mole* is always served with rice. *Tamales* are always served with beans. And who ever heard of chicken fried steak without mashed potatoes and gravy?

A Note
On The Menus
In This Book

A good friend of mine told me that appropriate food combinations were always her dilemma when she first started to cook: that she was the type to serve white rice and mashed potatoes at the same meal. Menus are always difficult to dream up, and even more so when you are not familiar with the cuisine, nor its traditions.

When I undertook the project of writing this book, I felt it was very important that the reader/chef have an idea how these foods would be presented. I would be remiss to give you a list of recipes outside the context of complete menus. It would be like scattering precious gems across a tabletop. Individually, each is enticing and beautiful, but only in the proper setting are the jewels seen in their best light.

Now, having said all that about menu combinations, let's review a few of the menus in this book: *Caldo de Mariscos* and Strawberry Pie? Fried Oysters with Tomato-Chipotle Sauce? *Puerco en Pipian* and Black Eyed Peas? Dove Pie and *Empanadas de Camote*? Seems a little mixed up, doesn't it? Well, that's life on the border, literally. We are undecided as to which way to go, which heritage hat to wear. For Texans, these menus are within the boundaries of what is typical. Our menus reflect our multi-faceted culture.

So if you want to serve *carne guisada* with mustard greens, or ham and *frijoles*, go right ahead. These pairings may seem unusual to some, but for us here in the Rio Grande Valley, and Texas, you'll make us feel right at home.

2

Table of Contents

Menus

Basics

Here are a few recipes, procedures and methods that will help you complete many of these menus

Corn Tortillas

Corn tortillas are not difficult, but they do take practice. One trick is to have two sheets of plastic to use with your tortilla press. Just cut a plastic baggie down to size. Place your ball of dough between the plastic sheets, then press with the tortilla press. Peel off the plastic, then lay your formed tortilla on the hot griddle. Make sure you don't cook them too long. Otherwise, they will dry out and be tough.

Instant corn tortilla masa mix, about 2 cups
hot water (a little over 1 cup)
salt to taste (optional)

Heat your griddle. In a large bowl, add masa, kneading in the water and a little salt. Add the water a bit at a time into the masa. The dough has sufficient water when it no longer sticks to your hands. Knead the dough for 1-2 minutes. Roll the dough into balls, about 2 inches in diameter. Using a tortilla press, press the balls into tortillas. Lay the tortillas on the hot griddle. Flip after 30 seconds of cooking. Flip again after 45 seconds. Remove from griddle after 30 more seconds.

Makes 16 tortillas

Tostadas
(Toasted Tortillas)

The traditional way of making tostadas is to fry tortillas in oil. Just heat some cooking oil in a skillet, and fry a cooked tortilla on each side until golden. Drain on paper towels. Sprinkle with salt or chile powder while still hot.

I rarely fry tostadas anymore, as I have found a fat free alternative to the fried tostada: The baked tostada.

To make baked tostadas: Heat the oven to 350°. Put the whole tortillas directly on the oven rack. Leave the oven door ajar slightly, to let the moisture escape. When the top side is browned a bit, flip them over. Remove tostada from oven when the tortilla is crispy, and both sides are brown. Be vigilant, as the tortillas will burn quickly.

You can fry or bake whole tortillas. If you want to make tortilla chips, cut the tortillas into quarters before frying or baking. Estimate two tortillas per person.

Store bought tortillas make the best tostadas. Homemade tortillas made into tostadas tend to be thicker in the center, so they don't crisp evenly, and can be chewy.

Flour Tortillas

I have only one thing to say about flour tortillas: practice. Getting the dough part right is not too hard. Below is the classic recipe Mexican women trade, measured in kilos. I converted it to cups for you, but to get consistent results, I would do it á la Mexicana and weigh the ingredients on a scale.

The hardest thing about flour tortillas is to get a round tortilla. Flour tortillas are rolled out with a rolling pin, not pressed with a tortilla press. The thinner the tortilla gets, the worse the situation becomes, and you do want your tortillas as thin as possible.

Frankly, the fact that you have undertaken the project of making homemade flour tortillas is admirable enough to outweigh any misshapen results. Make a game of it. Ask the kids what they imagine the shape of the tortilla to be, like looking for images in the clouds. You never know what you will see (Look Mom! It's Elvis!)

- **1 kilo flour (about 7 cups)**
- **2 tsp. baking powder**
- **1 tbsp. salt**
- **1/4 kilo vegetable shortening (about 1 1/3 cups)**
- **2 cups hot water**

In a large bowl, add the flour, baking powder, salt, and shortening. Knead well with your hands. Add in the water a little at a time until you have a smooth dough. Knead the dough for about 90 seconds, until elastic. Form the dough into 40 small patties. Return the patties to the mixing bowl, and allow to rest for 20 minutes. Heat up your griddle.

With a rolling pin, roll out the patties into tortillas, as thin and round as possible (this takes a lot of practice!). Place tortilla on the hot griddle. Flip tortilla to cook on the other side after 45 seconds. Flip again after 45 seconds. Flip one more time. The tortilla should puff up. Take tortilla off the griddle after 20 seconds and place in a clean towel to keep warm. Continue with the remaining dough.

Makes 40 tortillas

Mexican Style Beans / Refried Beans

Dried pinto or black beans (about 3 cups)
1 onion, chopped
1 tomato, chopped
2 whole cloves garlic
2 tbsp. chopped cilantro (optional)
2 whole serrano chilies
Salt to taste

Optional:
Some kind of meaty flavoring: salt pork, soup bone, ham, bacon, or a couple of bouillon cubes for a low-fat pot of beans.

Pick over beans, rinse well. Place in large pot and cover with water (at least five times the depth of the amount of dried beans). Add onion, tomato, garlic, meat flavor, cilantro, chilies and salt. Bring to a boil, then lower heat to simmer until tender, about three hours. Let cool fully before storing in refrigerator.

To refry: Add two tablespoons oil to a skillet and heat. Add cooked beans and mash with a potato masher. Simmer, then serve hot.

Notes on Beans:

Beans will keep for one week in the fridge. They freeze well, so save yourself a few hours in the future and freeze a batch. Make sure they are cold or room temperature before freezing. Freezing hot beans will allow the center of your bean container to stay at the optimum temperature for bacteria growth for a long time. And never reheat your beans continually. Only reheat what you think will be eaten. They will spoil very quickly, otherwise.

Some recommend soaking the beans overnight. I don't do this because they seem to spoil quicker. The bean cooker in your family may disagree with me. Never leave your beans out overnight to cool.

Watch your water level in your pot, and add more water if needed. Having too much water is not a bad thing. Having too little will cause burnt beans. Did someone light a cigarette? No, but check your beans. That is how they smell when they are burning.

Don't add cold water to hot beans, because then beans will burst. Boiling them at too high a temperature will do the same.

In spite of my lengthy notes on beans, they are one of the easiest things to cook.

Mexican Style Rice
(Traditional Method)

Pinch of whole cumin
pinch of black peppercorns
1 tomato
1 - 2 cloves garlic, peeled
2 tbsp. oil
1/2 onion, chopped
1 cup white rice
2 cups water or chicken broth
2 whole serrano chilies
1/2 cup minced green peas or diced carrots,
    or a combination of the two (optional)
salt to taste

In a *molcajete*, grind the cumin, peppercorns, tomato and garlic to make a salsa. Set aside. Sauté the onion in the oil until transparent in a heavy, lidded skillet. Add raw rice, sauté until rice turns opaque, without browning. Add water or chicken broth, salsa, chilies, salt, carrots and/or peas. Salt to taste. Allow rice to boil. Lower heat to simmering, cover tightly and simmer for 25-30 minutes. Do not remove lid during cooking process.

Serves 4

Mexican Style Rice
(Modern Method)

2 cups water or chicken broth
1 tomato
1 - 2 cloves garlic, peeled
2 tbsp. oil
1/2 onion, chopped
1 cup white rice
pinch of ground cumin
pinch of ground black pepper
2 whole serrano chilies
1/2 cup minced carrots or peas,
    or a combination of the two (optional)
salt to taste

In a blender, puree the water or chicken broth, tomato and garlic. Set aside. Sauté the onion in the oil until transparent in a heavy, lidded skillet. Add raw rice, sauté until rice turns opaque, without browning. Add puree, chilies, salt, carrots and/or peas, cumin and pepper. Salt to taste. Allow rice to boil. Lower heat to simmering, cover tightly and simmer for 25-30 minutes. Do not remove lid during cooking process.

Serves 4

Note: *Either rice recipe can easily be doubled or tripled.*

Pastry for pie crust:

Single 9" pie crust:
1 1/3 cups all purpose flour
1/3 cup shortening
pinch salt
3 - 4 tbsp. ice water

Double 9" pie crust:
2 cups all purpose flour
2/3 cup shortening
pinch salt
6 - 7 tbsp. ice water

In a large bowl, add in flour, shortening and salt. Knead with your hand until the mixture resembles a course meal. Add in the water one tablespoon at the time, until the dough can form a ball. Chill for one hour before rolling out.

If you need a baked pie shell, here is a trick to keep the crust from shrinking up when you bake it. Roll out the dough, line the pie plate and flute the edges. Prick holes in the pastry with a fork. Then place a sheet of aluminum foil over the pie crust. Press down to fit over crust, being careful of the fluted edges. Pour in either dried beans, or pie weights. Bake the pie crust for 10 minutes at 375˚. Remove crust from oven, remove foil with uncooked beans or pie weights, then bake pie crust for another 5-10 minutes. (Beans can still be cooked and eaten as usual.)

Ingredients

Notes on ingredients used in this book that may be unfamiliar to you

On Handling Chilies

Chilies are a super way to spice up foods, but they can set your hands, eyes, and throat on fire too, if you are not careful. If you need to handle a lot of chilies, remove their seeds, peel them, etc... you may want to use rubber gloves. I seeded a quarter pound of dried boiled chile chipotle once, and my burning hands kept me awake for quite some time. There is no remedy for chili burnt hands; only time (a couple of hours) will wear away the pain. Washing your hands only spreads the fire around. There are some peppers that are used in arthritis creams. I don't have arthritis, but those chilies certainly give my hands renewed life!

And for heaven's sake, don't rub your eyes! Touching your face or mouth can transfer the sensation as well. Watch the kids too. If you are a contact wearer and plan to work with chilies, either wear gloves or give into wearing your glasses that day.

What gives the chili its fire is a thin, gelatinous coating around the seed. The flavor is in the flesh; the fire is around the seed. So if you throw a couple of dried or fresh whole chilies into your dish, don't worry about your hands. If you boil or roast chilies and are removing the seeds, you may want to use gloves.

One last thing: When you roast or boil some chilies, you will sometimes get a sharp tickle in your throat. That is normal. It is just the ghost of the chili coming back for revenge. Chili aroma and vapor can be as irritating as the chili itself. Those with breathing problems may need to leave the room.

Roasting Poblano Chilies

Poblano chilies need to be roasted before use. Roasting cooks them a bit, and makes removal of the bitter peel easier. If you have a gas stove, just place a washed poblano chili directly on the flame. The chili will pop and blister. Turn with tongs to char evenly. Ashen spots are a sign that you have burned parts of the chili. Avoid burned spots, although your chili can still be salvaged for use. When the chili is evenly blackened, remove from the flame. With your fingers, peel the chili. If there are some bits that won't come off, use a knife to give them a scrape. Wash all the charred bits off with water. Slit the chili lengthwise. Remove the seeds, stem, and interior veins. You will be left with a tender, green, flat chili. Cut or use as directed in your recipe.

If you need more than three chilies, the easiest way to roast them is under your oven's broiler. Just place the washed chilies in a baking pan, and place them under the heated broiler. Turn the chilies periodically so that they char evenly. Peel, seed and stem the chilies as directed above.

Tomatillos

I am usually a stickler for buying the freshest ingredients possible. However, if you are using *tomatillos*, canned is better.

Tomatillos are a variety of small green tomatoes that have husks. After peeling off the husk, the sticky fruit must be washed well. Then the fruit must be boiled until tender, about 10 minutes. The *tomatillos* are now ready for use.

With canned *tomatillos*, the above preparation is omitted. All you do is open the can and the tomatillos are ready to go. There is very little difference in flavor.

Tomatillos come in 28oz cans, which are the perfect size for any recipe. One drained 28oz can of *tomatillos* equals 1 1/2 pounds of fresh *tomatillos*, or 2 cups of *tomatillo* puree.

Piloncillo

Piloncillo is made of sugar and invert sugar, and is traditionally cone shaped. It is sweeter than the equal amount of regular white sugar and has a distinctive caramel-like flavor. Because the cones are so solid and hard, *piloncillo* is usually combined with water to soften it or made into a syrup.

opalitos

A *nopal* is a prickly pear cactus, thus the diminutive, *nopalito*, just means "little cactus." The word *nopalito* is used mainly in referring to diced, cooked cactus. *Nopalitos* are added to everything from scrambled eggs, to elegant pasta dishes. In some of the trendy eateries around Texas, there are even *nopalito* margaritas. Obviously, it is a very versatile food.

There are several ways of buying *nopalitos*. One way is to buy them in packages, found in the fresh produce section of your supermarket. They have already been washed, dethorned, and diced. All you have to do is boil them in water until they turn from bright green to olive drab in color, about 15 minutes. Drain the water before using the cooked *nopalitos*. Like okra, cactus is a little gooey when cooked. If you like, just rinse the cooked cactus before you add it to your dish.

Another way of buying them is pre-cooked, packed in jars. You can find these in the ethnic food section. All you need to do with these *nopalitos* is drain the water and add the proper amount to your dish.

You can also go pick *nopalitos* out in the field. The new pads usually come out in late March, making *nopalitos* standard fare at Easter-time gatherings. Use a knife in each hand to harvest the pads: one to pierce and hold the pad, the other to cut the pad from the cactus plant.

To remove the thorns from the pad is easy. The trick is to not touch the cactus with your hands at all (have a pair of tweezers on hand, just in case). Using your two knives, hold the pad down on a flat surface. With the other knife, trim the thorns from the curved edge of the pad. Then, carefully nick the thorned pores from the surface of the pad. Turn pad over, and remove thorns from other side. Rinse well, then use as directed in your recipe.

amarindo

Tamarind or *tamarindo* is commonly used in Mexican sweets and drinks. It has a strong tangy flavor, and needs plenty of sugar.

Look for unbroken tamarind pods that are not too dried out, nor that show any evidence of bugs. Crack the shells off and remove veins before boiling the fruit. Boil in water until the fruit separates easily from the seeds, about 20 minutes. Press the fruit through a wire sieve to collect the tamarindo puree.

Tamarind is used throughout the African and Asian continents as well, so markets catering to those ethnic groups should have a good supply.

Tools

Notes on tools used
in this book that may
be unfamiliar to you

then pour the mixture directly from the *molcajete* into their simmering pan.

Molcajetes need to be "cured" before they are used. This is a long process, but in your lifetime, you will only have to do it once. A cured *molcajete* is a treasure you will keep forever. Grind uncooked rice grains in the *molcajete*, changing the ground rice for clean rice periodically. When the rice you are grinding is clean, and free of rock particles, your *molcajete* is ready for use. You may need to grind the rice in several sessions.

You will notice that I use a blender in many of the recipes. In Mexico, most households are turning from the *molcajete* to the blender to puree onions and tomatoes. However, you will still need the *molcajete* to grind spices.

 olcajete

A *molcajete* is a mortar made out volcanic rock, and is as common as a spoon in Mexican kitchens. The pestle is called the *tejolote*, or the *mano* (the hand). Regular mortar and pestle combinations can be used instead, but what is unique to the *molcajete* is the rough surface that aids in grating your spices.

If you would like to purchase a *molcajete*, make sure the bowl is ample enough to accommodate about two tomatoes. Do not get one so large that you can't move it around easily. Since they are carved out of stone, they are very heavy. Most people grind spices or garlic in the *molcajete*,

 olinillo

A *molinillo* is a wooden device used for making hot chocolate. It is a single piece of wood, carved to have a long, thin neck, a bulb at the base, and detached rings that dangle above the bulb. The neck of the *molinillo* is rubbed between your hands, much like the classic movie scenes of Native Americans, cave-dwellers and Boy Scouts starting fires with a stick.

To make Mexican style hot chocolate, you place a tablet of mexican chocolate in milk, and place the milk mixture on the stove to heat (see recipe, page 196). The spinning bulb of the *molinillo* is used to break up the solid chocolate tablet that is heating in milk. The dangling rings, as they spin, give the milk a nice froth.

The same frothing effect can also be achieved by adding the hot chocolate to a blender, and processing for a minute or two. *Molinillos*, however, are infinitely more charming, and are much easier to clean up.

Comal

A *comal* is a cast iron griddle commonly used for cooking tortillas in Mexico. Like anything made of cast-iron, it must be cured and cared for in a particular manner. When you first acquire your comal, wash it well, then heat it on your stove. Pour on some vegetable oil, about 2 tablespoons, and spread the oil with a folded paper towel. Repeat the coatings about two or three times. Cool the *comal*, wipe off the excess oil, then store. Before each usage of your *comal*, coat it with oil once in the same manner. When cleaning your *comal*, never scrub the surface, or clean it with harsh chemicals. Usually, a light cleaning with a damp towel will suffice.

Comals are very versatile. I use mine to make pancakes and grilled cheese sandwiches. You can roast your chilies on them as well. If you don't have a *comal*, a frying pan, or any other stovetop griddle will do.

Texas Chili Round-Up

Chile con Carne San Manuel

Nopalito Cornbread
[Cactus Cornbread]

Warm Apple Crisp

I love this chili recipe because it is so Texan. And it is a real time saver because the *chorizo* already has the proper flavors and spices for chili. Most chili making sessions turn into chemistry labs; mixing, stirring, brewing etc... If you enjoy spending hours in the kitchen, go for it. But this recipe takes about 20 minutes to mix up. Try it.

When I went away to school up East, there was one girl that kept bugging me about the amount of chili we ate down in "Tex-us." I said we didn't eat much chili in my neck of the woods, but she still gave me grief about what she perceived to be was my favorite dish. Slowly, I avenged myself by periodically telling stories about mountain oysters, *menudo, machitos, barbacoa, tripitas,* and the like. After a while, she didn't bring up the subject of food much.

Serve with: Variety of Mexican beers

Chile con Carne San Manuel

- 8 dried *chipotle* chilies
- 1 28oz can diced or whole tomatoes
- 4 lbs ground beef, or ground venison
- 12oz mexican style *chorizo*, casing removed
- 1 medium onion, chopped
- 3 cups whole pinto beans, cooked (homemade or canned)

In a small sauce pan, boil about 3 cups of water. When boiling, add the *chipotle* chilies. After about 10 minutes, check chilies to see if they are soft. Take out a chili from the water (you may want to use rubber gloves to handle chilies) and remove stem and seeds. Remove stems and seeds from remaining chilies, and rinse well. Place all seeded chilies in a blender, and add can of tomatoes. Puree well and salt to taste. (**Note**: *Leaving the chili seeds will make a your chile con carne spicier!*)

Brown chorizo and onion in large stew pot. Add ground venison or beef. When meat mixture is fully browned, add the rest of the can of tomatoes with juice, beans and pureed chilies. Salt to taste.

For best results, make a day ahead.

Serves 12

Nopalito Corn Bread

(Cactus Cornbread)

3/4 cup *nopalitos* (cactus bits – see Basics)
1/4 cup oil, shortening, or drippings
1 cup corn meal
1 cup all-purpose flour
1 - 2 tbsp. sugar (optional, more or less to taste)
1 tbsp. baking powder
1/2 tsp. salt
1 cup milk
1 egg, beaten
3/4 cup corn kernels, canned or fresh

Boil cactus in water until the pieces turn from bright green to dull green. Drain water and set aside.

Heat oven to 425°. Heat oil (shortening or drippings) in 10" oven proof skillet, or in a 8-9" baking pan for 3 minutes in oven.

Meanwhile, mix together dry ingredients in a bowl, add egg and milk; combine well. Add heated oil (shortening or drippings) and mix well. Add corn and cooked nopalito bits. Return batter to warmed skillet and bake for 20-25 minutes, or until a wooden pick inserted in the center comes out clean.

This cornbread can also be made in muffin or stick form, by not heating the oil, but adding it (in liquid form) to the batter. Pour into greased or paper lined muffin tins or into well greased corn stick forms. Bake at 425° for 15-20 minutes or until golden brown.

Warm Apple Crisp

Filling:	Topping:
6 Granny Smith Apples	3/4 cup butter, softened
juice of 1 lemon	1 cup flour
1/4 cup flour	1 cup rolled oats
1/2 cup sugar	1 tsp. cinnamon
2 tsp. cinnamon	1 cup sugar
2 tbsp. brandy (optional)	

Preheat oven to 350°. Peel and slice apples into a bowl with the lemon juice. Add in remaining filling ingredients. Toss to coat evenly. Place mixture in a 2 quart baking dish.

Combine topping ingredients in a separate bowl. Mixture should resemble small peas. Sprinkle topping over apples. Bake for 45 minutes, until top is golden brown.

Serves 8

Autumn Barbeque

Pollo en Achiote
(Chicken in Achiote Marinade)
Pork Ribs with Two Pepper Sauce
Grilled Sourdough with Herbed Chevre
Fresh Grapefruit Pie

Achiote is a wonderful, little known spice. My sister-in-law introduced me to *achiote* while I was visiting her in Saltillo, Coahuila, Mexico. She had fried some pork chops that had marinated in the *condimento de achiote*. They had a bright orange color and a tangy taste from the vinegar.

Achiote is the annatto seed used in coloring cheese yellow. You can make your own *recado de achiote* by grinding whole anatto seeds with various spices, but the commercial preparations are excellent and convenient to use. I pick mine up when I'm in Mexico, but for those of you who live away from the border should be able to find spice preparations with *achiote* in the ethnic food section of your market.

If you have an ornamental sour orange tree, now is the time to utilize some of the fruit. You can mix your *condimento de achiote* with either sour orange juice, or vinegar. Do not use regular sweet orange juice, as it lacks the essential tangy flavor.

One of the glories of our Rio Grande Valley autumns is the harvest of the Ruby Red grapefruit. They are what every little grapefruit should aspire to be. Sweet, juicy and deep red on the inside, blushing like a peach on the outside. Use them for your pie if you can find them.

Serve with: beans, rice, tortillas or bread, salad

Pollo en Achiote

(Chicken in Achiote Marinade)

4 chicken breasts, with ribs, skin removed
1 oz *condimento de achiote*
1 tsp. dried oregano
salt and pepper
1/2 cup vinegar or sour orange juice (not sweet)

Place chicken in shallow glass dish. Combine achiote, spices, and vinegar in separate bowl. Pour over chicken and let marinate for 30 minutes in the refrigerator. Grill chicken over hot coals or gas grill until well cooked, about 30 minutes.

Serves 4

Pork Ribs with Two Pepper Barbecue Sauce

5 lbs pork loin back (baby back) ribs
salt, pepper, or favorite seasoning mixture
        (I like Cavender's Greek seasoning)

Sauce:
2 tbsp. olive oil
1 onion, chopped
1 large rib celery, chopped
1/2 red bell pepper, seeded and sliced
2 long red dried chilies (*chile de arbol*),
        stem removed, seeds reserved
2 cloves garlic, minced
1/4 cup vinegar
1 cup ketchup
2 tbsp. Worcestershire sauce
1 tbsp. dry prepared mustard
1/4 cup brown sugar

Heat oven to 350°. In a large baking pan, season ribs. Bake for one hour.

Meanwhile, in a saucepan, saute onion, celery, and bell pepper in oil. Add dried chilies, and a few of the seeds (the more seeds you add, the spicier the resulting sauce). Add the garlic, and saute for about 3 more minutes. Add remaining ingredients, and simmer for 5 minutes. Remove from heat, and let stand for 10 minutes.

Puree mixture in food processor, making sure no large pieces remain.

Finish cooking ribs on a heated barbecue grill, about 10 minutes. Cover ribs with sauce before serving, or serve sauce on the side.

Serves 4

Note: *This sauce is not too spicy for children, but you can omit the chili and/or the chili seeds altogether if you wish. If it is not barbecue weather outside, bake the ribs about 15 minutes longer, then finish them under the broiler.*

Grilled Sourdough with Herbed Chevre

Select your favorite dense bread (I like homemade sourdough) and slice in half inch slices. Brush one side with olive oil. Place oiled side down on heated barbecue grill. Let toast for about 2 minutes. Brush top side with oil, then turn to toast other side. Serve with an herbed chevre (goat cheese).

Fresh Grapefruit Pie

1 pre-baked 9" pie shell (see Basics)

Filling:
5 - 6 fresh grapefruit, enough for 5 cups of fruit
1 cup fresh strawberries
1 cup water
3 tbsp. cornstarch, sifted
3/4 cup sugar
whipped cream

Section grapefruit, removing membrane and leaving slices whole or in large pieces. Set aside.

In a small saucepan, combine water and strawberries. Bring to a boil, crushing strawberries. Boil for 2-3 minutes. Sieve mixture, reserving the liquid and pressing the pulp through the strainer. Discard remaining pulp. In same saucepan, return berry juice, adding the cornstarch and the sugar. Stir continuously, until clear and thick.

Spread about 1/4 cup of the gel in the pie shell. With a slotted spoon, carefully place a third of the grapefruit sections in the prepared pie crust (do not add any collected juice from the grapefruit sections). Spread another 1/4 cup of gel on top of grapefruit, and continue layering fruit and gel, ending with a layer of the gel on top. Chill for about three hours before serving. Serve with whipped cream.

Serves 6

Huachinango a la Veracruzana

Huachinango a la Veracruzana
(Red Snapper, Veracruz Style)

Chilled Cream of Avocado Soup

Polvorones de Tequila
(Tequila Sugar Cookies)

Agua de Sandia
(Refreshment of Watermelon)

Huachinango a la Veracruzana is a spectacular dish for guests. The colors in this menu are dazzling, and the preparation is not at all difficult. The presentation of the whole fish will fill you with the same pride that the perfectly browned Thanksgiving turkey does upon arrival at the dining table.

The chilled soup is wonderfully refreshing, and a bit lighter than other avocado soup recipes in that it uses whole milk, instead of heavy cream.

I promised I wouldn't tell this story, but here I go anyway. My sister-in-law, Luisa, and I were making the tequila sugar cookies one afternoon. We made a mistake in the measurements, and since we were testing the recipe, I insisted we do the whole thing over again. That meant we would end up with 24 dozen cookies. So we got squared away for the second batch, and having just put a pan in the oven, we were standing there chatting. All of a sudden, the door of the oven blew open, a flame shot out, and then it closed itself again. Luisa asked me what I had done, and I said that I had done nothing. What we finally figured out was that after 2 hours of baking cookies, the tequila fumes had built up in the oven, and had ignited.

Serve with: black beans, white rice, and corn tortillas

Huachinango a la Veracruzana

(Red Snapper, Veracruz Style)

One 4 - 6 lb Red Snapper

Sauce:
4 limes
3 lbs tomatoes
1/3 cup olive oil
1 large onion, sliced
4 clove garlic, minced
3 tbsp. capers
2 bay leaves
2/3 cup olives stuffed with pimentos
2 pickled jalapeño peppers, seeded, cut into strips
3 sprigs fresh marjoram (or 1 tsp. dried)
3 sprigs fresh thyme (or 1 tsp. dried)
3 sprigs fresh oregano leaves (or 1 tsp. dried)

Make sure your fish has been cleaned, and all scales removed. Do not remove tail, head, or any fins. Rinse and place in non-metallic casserole dish, large enough to accommodate the entire fish, from mouth to tail, and the sauce. Squeeze the juice of the limes over the fish, and sprinkle with 1-2 teaspoons of salt. Let fish marinate in the fridge for one hour. Meanwhile, peel and seed tomatoes (see note). Chop tomatoes into cubes, and set aside. Heat oven to 350°.

Heat olive oil in a large pan, then add onion. Add minced garlic to pan. Saute, but don't let garlic burn. After 1 minute of sauteing, add chopped tomatoes, and remaining ingredients. Salt to taste. Let simmer until sauce reduces a bit, about 15 minutes. Pour sauce over fish, and place in preheated oven for one hour.

Serve immediately with tortillas and white rice.

Serves 4

Note: *To peel tomatoes, plunge tomato into boiling water for 15 seconds. Remove, and pierce tomato with knife. The peel should come off easily. If not, return to water briefly and try again. To seed tomatoes, after peeling, cut in half horizontally through middle. Squeeze half gently, and seeds should release. By the way, if you're in a rush, you don't have to peel and seed your tomatoes. Your dish will not be as pretty, or elegant, but will taste just as good. And, you'll have increased the fiber in your diet slightly. If you have a fish larger than 6 lbs, just make more sauce. Or less, for a smaller fish.*

You can make the sauce one day in advance, simmering only for a few minutes, then cooling to room temperature, and storing in the refrigerator overnight. All tomato dishes taste better the second day, after the flavors have "married." Just skip the fish preparation until you are ready to cook your meal. This is a great idea if you are headed to the beach to go snapper fishing.

Chilled Cream of Avocado Soup

2 cups chicken broth
1 carrot
1 rib celery with leaves
1/4 cup chopped leeks, well washed
2 bay leaves
3 ripe avocados
2 cups whole milk
1/4 tsp. white pepper
1/4 tsp. cayenne pepper

Boil chicken broth with carrot, celery, leeks and bay leaves, about 15 minutes. Let cool. Remove bay leaves.

Peel and seed avocados, and place in the bowl of a food processor or in the container of a blender. Remove vegetables from the chicken broth, and add to bowl as well. Reserve broth. Begin to puree avocados and vegetables, adding broth through the top of the processor/ blender. Blend until very smooth. Pour puree into a separate bowl. Add milk and both peppers. Chill at least two hours or overnight, then serve.

Serves 8

Polvorones de Tequila

(Tequila Sugar Cookies)

Cookie:
5 cups flour
1 1/4 cups sugar
3/4 cup tequila
1 tbsp. ground cinnamon (freshly ground, if possible)
1 1/2 tsp. baking powder
2 3/4 cups shortening

Sugar topping:
1 cup sugar
1 tbsp. ground cinnamon (freshly ground, if possible)

Preheat oven to 350°. Combine cookie ingredients in large mixing bowl. Knead dough together with hands. When the dough is well combined, allow to rest for 15 minutes. Combine sugar and cinnamon for topping in a shallow dish.

On a floured surface, roll cookie dough out in a 1/4 inch thickness. Cut into 2 inch circles, with a cookie cutter or a small glass. Arrange on an ungreased cookie sheet, and bake for 12-15 minutes, until pale golden in color, and firm to the touch. Roll in sugar topping while hot.

Makes 12 dozen

A gua de Sandía

(Refreshment of Watermelon)

Watermelon (or cantaloupe, honeydew, any melon)
water
sugar to taste

Seed melon, remove rind, and cut into chunks.
Pureé watermelon in food processor. Strain if
you like, although many people prefer the pulp.
Add enough water for a thin drink, but don't
dilute the flavor. Add sugar if needed. Serve
over ice.

Mixed Grill

Mixed Grill of Beef
and Venison Sausage

Grilled Vegetables

Roasted Potatoes

Pecan Mustard Green Beans

Peach Brandy

Much of this menu must be done well in advance, but once these preparations are done, the meal should only take an hour to assemble and serve.

Here on the ranch, we have been blessed with a resurgence in the population of the white-tail deer. Venison is always on the menu in the winter, and makes occasional appearances from the freezer in the spring (if it lasts that long!). Venison sausage is very popular here. Most folks send their venison to a professional processor to make their sausage. I don't think any of them know how easy and fun it is to make the sausage at home. With a minimum of equipment, expense, and knowledge, you can amaze your friends with your sausage wizardry.

Those in search of the perfectly crunchy potato need search no more. These roasted potatoes have received rave reviews. And you must use olive oil to get the best flavor and texture.

As refreshing as dessert is after a meal, sometimes it is just as refreshing not to have dessert. This menu is a bit heavy, so you can end on a lighter note with a nice peach brandy, a little fresh fruit, and maybe a bit of sharp cheese.

Mixed Grill of Beef and Venison Sausage

Beef
For the beef, select your favorite cuts of beef. I love little filets, about 2 inches thick, with no bacon wrappers. Whatever you choose, make sure it is on the thick side, with a fair amount of marbling.

Venison Sausage
Your pork can be fairly fatty, as venison has virtually no fat. This sausage will be about 50% fat, and you will be surprised how lean it is compared to commercial sausage. I do not recommend cooking any of your sausage before it has aged 24 hours with the spices. The spices need time to "marry" before you can get a good idea of how it will taste when served. If you like, fry a little, and try it before you put them in their casings. Adjust the flavors to your liking at that time.

Make sure your meat grinder has sausage stuffing capabilities. You can usually buy the necessary accessory attachments at the hardware store. I have a mechanical sausage stuffer. It is a cast iron elbow-shaped pipe with a plunger. If you don't want to invest in any sausage equipment, ask your butcher if he/she can stuff your sausage into casings for you.

By the way, collect all your spices before you even start with the grinding, and measure them into a small bowl. That way, when they are needed, you don't have to slow down to play the chemical engineer.

6 lbs venison
5 lbs pork picnic shoulder, rind and bone removed

Spices:
2 tsp. cayenne pepper
2 tsp. thyme
2 tbsp. rubbed sage
2 tsp. ground allspice
1 tbsp. mustard seeds
1 tbsp. ground black pepper
8 cloves garlic, pressed
2 tbsp. salt
4 tbsp. sugar
1 cup brandy

Enough sausage casing for 12 lbs sausage

Make sure venison is well prepared (no sinew or gristle) and that your pork is not too lean. Grind both meats through the coarse plate in your meat grinder. Place all meat in a large basin. Add all spices and brandy. Mix well by kneading mixture with hands.

Prepare your meat grinder for stuffing sausage. Make sure casing is clean and has no holes. Stuff sausage as directed by the meat grinder's manufacturer. Freeze or cook sausage within 24 hours.

Makes 12 lbs sausage

Grilled Vegetables

Select from the list below, calculating about two pounds of mixed vegetables per person. That may sound like a lot, but remember that they will lose liquid while cooking.

Onions - Cut into two inch thick rounds. A wooden skewer will help rings stay together.

Eggplant - Cut into 3/4 inch rounds or lengthwise into slabs

Peppers - Bell pepper of all colors, seeded and cut into quarters

Chilies - fresh green chiles, skewered, with stem intact

Squash - zucchini, banana, tatuma - sliced lengthwise in half, or in 1 1/2 inch thick slabs.

Mushrooms - Portobello and snow white mushrooms - make sure they are well cleaned.

After selecting and preparing your desired vegetables, slather them in vegetable oil. Grill these before or while you grill your meat.

nion Mustard Dressing

1/2 cup Dijon mustard with seeds
6 tbsp. apple cider vinegar
2/3 cup grated onion
salt and pepper
1 1/2 cups olive oil

Whisk mustard, vinegar, onion, salt and pepper in a bowl. Slowly add oil, whisking continuously. Make sure dressing is well mixed before using. Makes about 2 cups.

oasted Potatoes

2 lbs baby red potatoes
1 1/2 cups Onion Mustard dressing

Preheat your oven to 450°. Wash potatoes, and cut in quarters (do not peel). In a large baking pan, add potatoes, and pour dressing over top, tossing potatoes to coat evenly. Place in heated oven for 30 minutes, turning over once during cooking. Turn oven broiler on, and leave potatoes under broiler for 30-45 minutes more, turning potatoes over to brown evenly.

Serves 8

ecan Mustard Green Beans

- 2 lbs green beans, trimmed
- 1/2 cup Onion Mustard dressing
- 1/2 cup pecans, finely chopped

- Cook green beans for 5 minutes in boiling salted water. Drain water well, then return green beans to pot. Add dressing and pecans, and toss to coat evenly. Serve immediately.

Serves 8

each Brandy

- 15 peaches, not over ripe, nor under ripe
- 1 liter brandy
- 1 1/2 cups sugar

Wash the peaches well, rubbing the skin to remove the fuzz. Place in a large glass or ceramic container, and pour brandy in. Cover tightly, and allow to macerate for ten days. After ten days, remove cover, and add sugar. Cover tightly again, and allow to age for 60 more days. Stir occasionally.

At the end of 60 days, remove peaches, and filter liquor through a coffee filter, to remove any dregs. Store in an old wine bottle or a decorative glass bottle in a cool, dark cabinet.

Flautas

Flautas
(Flute Shaped Tacos)

Aqua de Tamarindo
(Refreshment of Tamarind)

Almond Scented Macaroons

Flautas are a safe menu to serve, no matter what crowd is coming over. Everybody loves them. The unfried *flautas* can be frozen until you need them. They can be fried after a minimum of thawing. If you have a thundering herd of vegetarians headed your way, substitute refried beans, cheese, or strips of chilies for the chicken filling.

When you select your tamarind beans, make sure they have no bugs, that the outer shells are mostly intact, and that the shell breaks cleanly away from a moist internal pod of fruit. *Agua de Tamarindo* does not have an exciting color like most of the beverages on the market today, and it does need a stir every now and then, but those who try it love it.

Serve with: rice and beans

Flautas

(Flute Shaped Tacos)

50 corn tortillas, either fresh or store bought
4 chicken breasts, with ribs (enough for 5 cups
    of cooked chicken)
1 onion, halved
1 clove garlic
1 serrano chile, whole
1 bay leaf
1 1/2 lbs fresh tomatillos, or 1 28oz can of
    tomatillos, water drained
1 ripe avocado, peeled and seeded
2 cups oil for frying
1/2 cup Mexican sour cream, or creme fraiche
2 cups shredded lettuce
1 - 2 tomatoes, diced
1/2 onion, sliced thinly
1 cup queso fresco, or feta cheese, crumbled

Boil chicken with onion, garlic, chile and bay leaf, until chicken is cooked. Remove from heat. Allow chicken to cool on a plate, and reserve broth for another meal. When chicken is cool, remove skin and bones, and shred finely.

Husk and wash tomatillos (no washing, husking or cooking needed if using canned tomatillos). Place in saucepan and cover with water. Bring to a boil. When tomatillos turn from bright to dull olive green, they are cooked, about 10 minutes. Drain water from pan. Place cooked or canned tomatillos with avocado in a blender. Puree well. Salt to taste and set aside.

Wrap tortillas in a cloth towel, and heat for 2 minutes in the microwave. This will make the tortillas pliable for rolling into flautas. Place about 2 tablespoons of the chicken in a line to one side of the center of the tortilla. Start rolling up the tortilla on the side where you placed the shredded chicken, and roll into a tightly formed flute. Place in a baking pan until all the flutes have been rolled, keeping them together tightly, with the seam side down.

Heat oil in a large pan. Fry flutes, seam side down, until they start to brown, about 8 minutes. Try to keep them close together, so they will not unroll. Turn once and brown for 2-3 more minutes. Remove from oil, and drain on paper towels. Continue frying remaining flutes.

Place cooked flautas on a serving platter. Pour green sauce over, then drizzle with sour cream. Top with lettuce, tomatoes, onions and crumbled cheese. Serve immediately.

Serves 8

Note: *If your flautas keep unrolling, your tortillas need to be hotter. If that fails, try toothpicks to keep them together while frying. Remove toothpicks before serving. If you are serving these to guests, you can fry the flautas in advance, and hold them for a short time in a warm oven. If you can't find mexican sour cream or creme fraiche, take some regular sour cream, and thin it with some milk. Do this at the last minute, as the sour cream will thicken again fairly quickly.*

gua de Tamarindo

(Refreshment of Tamarind)

1 lb tamarind pods
3/4 cup sugar
water

Shell tamarind pods, and remove the veins. Place fruit pod in saucepan, and discard shell. Boil in 3-4 cups water, until soft, about 20 minutes. Strain water through mesh sieve. Press fruit pods, straining fruit through sieve. Seeds and fiber will remain in sieve, while fruit presses through. This will render approximately 3 cups of concentrate. You may wish to puree the concentrate in blender, as this will make the resulting beverage a bit more homogenous.

Add sugar and enough water to make 2 1/2 to 3 quarts of beverage. Adjust sugar and water to taste.

Note: *Agua de Tamarindo tends to separate, with the fruit on the bottom, and the water on top. Giving the concentrated tamarindo a spin in the blender seems to solve this problem, but it will still separate a bit.*

lmond Scented Macaroons

- 3 egg whites, brought to room temperature
- pinch salt
- 1 tsp. almond extract
- 1 cup sugar
- 3 cups grated coconut

Heat oven to 325°. Beat egg whites with an electric mixer until peaks form. Add salt almond extract and sugar slowly, until mixture shows well formed peaks. Fold in coconut. Drop in 2 inch wide dollops onto greased cookie sheet. Bake for 20 minutes, or until lightly golden.

Kikín Duck

Kikín Duck

Salsa de Chile Pasilla

Picado de Cebolla y Cilantro
(Onions and Cilantro Relish)

Pistachio Ice Cream

One of my first attempts in exotic cooking was to make a Chinese style Peking Duck. I was amazed by how easy it was to prepare. Musing on what recipes to create for this book, I thought back to this recipe, and wondered how we could do duck South Texas style. I tried this duck various ways, but the best way is the Chinese way: air dried for a few hours, then baked in the oven. The skin of the duck turns out perfectly brown and crisp, and the meat succulent.

The sauces and tortillas changed the nationality of this duck dish. I created a sauce with chile pasilla that is mildly spicy, and combined it with an onion and cilantro relish. The chipotle chilies in this recipe are not dried, but canned, in a spicy adobo sauce. These can be found near the canned jalapeño peppers in your supermarket. Flour tortillas replace the mu shu pancakes usually served with the Chinese version of this duck.

If you can't find shelled pistachios for the ice cream, just sit down with your family and friends, and shell one pound of pistachios. Everyone will take pride in the finished product, and you'll have made a memory.

Serve with: flour tortillas, rice and beans, spinach salad

Kikín Duck

2 domestic ducks, giblets removed

Marinade:
6 cups water
1/4 cup onion, chopped
3 tbsp. honey
3 tbsp. white wine
1" cube fresh ginger, peeled
3 tbsp. cornstarch
1/2 cup water

Cut neck flap from ducks, if desired. Tie a strong twine around the wings of each duck, pulling the wings back towards the spine. Use this string to hang the ducks, so that the skin can air dry for about three hours. Place in front of a fan or an air vent to dry more quickly.

Combine 6 cups water, onion, honey, white wine and ginger. Simmer mixture. Mix together cornstarch with 1/2 cup water, and add to water mixture. When mixture is barely boiling, dip in whole duck, allowing body cavity to fill with liquid.

Let mixture drain off of duck, then repeat dipping. Hang to dry for another 2-3 hours.

Heat oven to 350°. Bake ducks on a broiler pan for 2 hours. Serve immediately with Chile Pasilla Sauce and Picado de Cebolla y Cilantro.

Salsa de Chile Pasilla

- 2 pasilla chilies
- 2 guajillo chilies
- 2 roma tomatoes or 1 regular tomato, chopped
- 1/4 onion, chopped
- 1 garlic
- 3 chipotle chilies, canned, in adobo sauce
- Salt to taste
- oil

Boil the pasilla and guajillo chilies in a small amount of water until tender. Drain water and remove chile stems. Combine chilies, tomatoes, onion, garlic, and chile chipotle in a blender container. Puree well and salt to taste. Add enough water to facilitate blending (about 1/4 cup).

In a skillet, heat about 2 tablespoons of oil. When hot, add in chili puree. Simmer sauce until reduced and thickened, about 20 minutes. Serve warm.

Makes about 1 1/2 cups

Picado de Cebolla y Cilantro

(Onion and Cilantro Relish)

1 1/2 cups white onion, very finely chopped
1/2 cup cilantro, very finely chopped
salt

Combine ingredients, and salt to taste.

Makes about 2 cups

# Pistachio Ice Cream

2 cups shelled pistachios (1 lb. with shells will render
   2 cups unshelled)
3 tbsp. butter
1/4 cup cornstarch
2 1/4 cups sugar
1/2 tsp. salt
5 cups whole milk
4 eggs
4 cups heavy cream
1 tbsp. almond extract
1 tbsp. vanilla extract
8 drops green food coloring (optional)
15 lbs crushed ice (for ice cream freezer)
salt for ice cream freezer

- Coarsely chop pistachios. Melt butter in a skillet, and saute pistachios for 8-10 minutes, until toasted. Set aside.

- Combine cornstarch, sugar and salt in a large saucepan. Add milk and mix well. Cook mixture for 15-20 minutes, until thickened, stirring constantly. Remove from heat.

- In a separate bowl, beat eggs with an electric hand mixer. While mixing, add in hot milk mixture, one spoonful at a time, until you have added approximately 1 1/2 cups of the mixture. Return egg mixture to the saucepan containing the remaining thickened milk, combining well. Return to heat and cook for 1-2 minutes. Remove from heat. Transfer to a mixing bowl, cover, and chill for 2 hours.

- Combine chilled mixture with the cream, extracts and coloring. Mix well, then add sauteed pistachios. Pour mixture into the canister of a 4 quart ice cream freezer. Freeze according to the manufacturer's directions. After the ice cream has been frozen, store ice cream in the freezer overnight, allowing it to "ripen."

Makes 1 gallon

Chuletas Verdes con Cebolla

Chuletas Verdes con Cebolla
(Green Pork Chops with Onions)

Monedas y Pepitas
(Carrot Coins with Pumpkin Seeds)

Pineapple Pie

These pork chops were one of my grandmother's favorite recipes. The sour flavor of the tomatillos is a great compliment to the rich texture of the pork. (You can also grill the chops to cook them, instead of frying.)

Check out the recipe for *tepache* before you throw away the rind of your pineapple.

Serve with: rice, beans and corn tortillas.

Chuletas Verdes con Cebolla
(Green Pork Chops with Onions)

3 lbs pork chops with bones
oil

Sauce:
1 onion, sliced
2 1/4 lbs fresh tomatillos,
    or two 28oz cans prepared whole tomatillos
1 clove garlic
2 whole serrano chilies
salt to taste

If using fresh tomatillos, husk and wash them, then place the tomatillos in a saucepan, covering them with water. Bring water to boil, and allow to simmer for about 10 minutes, or until tomatillos turn from bright green to a dull olive color. Drain water, and set aside.

If using canned tomatillos, drain water, then set aside.

In a large skillet, fry the pork chops in a small amount of oil, about 8-10 minutes on each side. Make sure the pork is well cooked. Drain on paper towels. Place in a large oven proof casserole dish.

Heat oven to 350°. Place tomatillos with garlic in a blender and puree. Set aside. In a clean skillet, fry the onion in a bit of oil. Add in tomatillo puree, and whole chilies. Salt to taste, and allow to simmer for 10 minutes, until slightly reduced. Pour sauce over pork chops, and bake in oven for 30 minutes.

Serves 6

Monedas y Pepitas
(Carrot Coins with Pumpkin Seeds)

1 1/2 lbs carrots, peeled and cut into thin circles
3 tbsp. olive oil
1/4 onion, sliced
1/2 cup raw, unsalted, shelled pumpkin seeds
2 cloves garlic, minced
salt to taste

Boil carrots until easily pierced with a fork. Drain the water, and set aside.

In a skillet, heat the olive oil. Saute the onion until translucent. Add in the pumpkin seeds, and saute until the seeds start to pop. Add in cooked carrots, minced garlic, and salt. Toss to coat the carrots well.

Serves 6

Pineapple Pie

- Pastry for a double crust 9" pie (see Basics)

- Filling:
- 1 pineapple, peeled, cored and chopped well (about 4 cups fruit)
- 3 tbsp. quick cooking tapioca
- pinch salt
- 3/4 cup sugar
- juice of one lemon
- 1 tbsp. butter

Line a 9" pie plate with half of the pastry. Heat oven to 400°. Mix together pineapple, tapioca, sugar, salt and lemon juice. Let mixture stand for 15 minutes. Pour into pie shell, and dot top of filling with butter. Cover with top crust, and decorate with extra pastry. Bake for 45 minutes. Top with foil in oven if crust begins to brown too much. Cool, then serve.

Serves 8

Dove Pie

Dove Pie

Mashed Potatoes and Turnips

Turnip Greens

Empanadas de Camote
(Sweet Potato Turnovers)

Dove pie is an adaptation of the English savory pie, using our local fare. The usual way of preparing doves is to bread and deep fry them. I prefer dove pie because it is elegant, travels well, and has so many possibilities for a beautiful presentation.

Anyone who has ever cooked game knows how tough the meat can be at times. By cutting the cooked dove meat into small pieces, we have eliminated that problem entirely.

I love turnips, but they are more easily served to the first-time turnip eater if their flavor is diluted a bit with potatoes. I threw in the turnip green recipe because when you buy turnips, you get a free bunch of turnip greens. You might as well enjoy them. Make sure you boil the greens long enough to mellow their bitter flavor.

Dove Pie

- Pastry for a 9" double crust pie

- Stock and meat:
- 10 - 12 doves, cleaned
- 2 ribs celery, with leaves, chopped
- 1 carrot, chopped

- Filling:
- 1 rib celery, chopped
- 1/3 cup onion, chopped
- 1 tbsp. butter
- 1 tbsp. flour
- 1 1/2 cups dove stock
- 1/2 tsp. Worcestershire sauce
- 3/4 cup fresh or frozen peas
- 3/4 cup finely chopped carrots
- 1 cup sliced mushrooms

Boil doves in a stock pot along with celery and carrot, about 30 minutes, until well cooked. Remove doves from broth, reserving 1 1/2 cups of the broth. Allow doves to cool, then debone and shred the meat. Set aside.

Line a 9" pie plate with half of the pastry. Set aside. Roll out other half of pastry for top.

Heat oven to 400°. In a large pan, heat butter, and brown carrots, celery, and onions. Add flour and mix well. Add in stock, and allow flour to completely blend with stock. Add Worcestershire sauce, and allow mixture to thicken. Add in peas, mushrooms and dove meat, and allow to simmer for 10 minutes.

Pour dove filling into prepared pie plate. Cover with other half of rolled pastry, and seal and decorate edges. Bake for 35-40 minutes. Allow to cool slightly before serving.

Serves 6

 # ashed Potatoes and Turnips

1 lb turnips
2 lbs potatoes
2 tbsp. butter
1/4 cup whole milk
salt to taste

Remove tops and peel turnips, and chop in quarters. Peel and pare potatoes, and quarter. Place in a large pot, cover with water. Boil until tender, about 30 minutes.

Drain water well. Add butter and milk, and mash potatoes and turnips with a potato masher. Make sure no lumps remain. Salt to taste.

Serves 8

 # urnip Greens

3 large bunches turnip greens
3 slices bacon, chopped
2 tsp. molasses
salt to taste

Wash the greens well in water, removing any grit. Chop into inch wide strips. Boil the greens in a large pot of water with the bacon, molasses and salt for 25-30 minutes. Serve greens with some of the "pot likker" (cooking liquid).

Serves 8

Empanadas de Camote

(Sweet Potato Turnovers)

Dough:
1 3/4 cups shortening
4 cups flour
1/4 cup sugar
1 tsp. salt
1 egg
1/2 cup water
1 tbsp. vinegar

Filling:
2 lbs sweet potatoes
2 sticks cinnamon
1/2 - 1 cup sugar, to taste

For the dough: Knead the shortening into the flour, sugar and salt with your hands. Add in egg, water, and vinegar, mixing well. Form dough into a ball, wrap in plastic, and chill for one hour.

Meanwhile, wash sweet potatoes well, and cut into large chunks. Boil sweet potatoes with the cinnamon until the potatoes are easily pierced with a fork. Drain water from pot. Remove cinnamon sticks. After the sweet potatoes have cooled, peel, then puree with an electric hand mixer. Add in sugar, as desired.

Heat your oven to 350°. Form the dough into 30 balls. Using a tortilla press or a rolling pin, flatten the dough into circles. Fill with 1 tablespoon of the mashed sweet potatoes. Do not overfill. Fold dough over the filling to form a half circle. Pinch edges together. Place on an ungreased cookie sheet. When all empanadas are formed, crimp edges where empanada is sealed with a fork. Bake for 20-25 minutes, until browned.

Makes 30 empanadas

Fajita Buffet

Fajitas

Queso con Rajas
(Cheese with Chili Strips)

Salsa Chimichurri

Arroz con Leche
(Rice Pudding)

Almost every gathering I attend serves this meal. It is easy to serve a crowd, and not terribly expensive. In the Rio Grande Valley, where I live, this would qualify as our regional "signature" dish.

The Salsa Chimichurri is from Argentina. I have seen several variations of this sauce. This sauce is definitely for garlic lovers.

Serve with: Rice, beans, your favorite salsa and tortillas

 ajitas

- *Fajitas* need a bit of explaining. The word *faja*, in Spanish, means a sash, or girdle-like band, thus a *fajita* is a <u>little</u> girdle. Therefore, *fajitas* are a cut of meat, like the loin or rump. "*Fajita*" does not mean a cooking style.

- *Fajitas* initially became popular because they were cheap. Working folks could afford this cut of beef to feed their large families. Now the foodies have discovered *fajitas*, and their price has skyrocketed, beyond that of a good steak.

- Keep in mind, chicken and fish do not have the anatomy that necessitates a *fajita*, therefore, chicken, shrimp, and fish *fajitas* are misnomers.

- There are two types of *fajitas*: One is the "inside" *fajita* which comes from the inside of the rib and and the "outside" *fajita* which comes from the outside of the rib.

- The "outside" *fajita* is the diaphragm muscle, and has a thick outer membrane on both sides. This membrane keeps the meat moist and tender while grilling, and therefore makes the "outside" *fajita* the choice of *fajita* connoisseurs. This membrane, however, is usually peeled off before serving, which can be a bit messy and inconvenient.

- Since the "inside" *fajita* has no membrane, they are also known as "skinless" *fajitas*. They need no other preparation other than grilling, and for that reason, are quite convenient and quick to prepare.

Even though there are quite a few fancy recipes for *fajita* marinades and sauces, the classic way to prepare them is grilled over a wood fire. Gas grills and charcoal work very well, or in a pinch, you could broil or pan fry them. However, in my neck of the woods, *fajitas* are the classic outdoor barbecue choice.

Four pounds should be enough to feed 8 people. Season them with salt, pepper, or your favorite spice blend, such as garlic salt or lemon pepper. Grill over a low heat for about 30 minutes. Cooking time will depend on the thickness of the meat. Cook them to your desired degree of doneness. And remember, when slicing the *fajitas*, cut them across the grain of the meat, not in the direction of the grain.

Queso con Rajas

(Cheese with Chile Strips)

24 oz queso asadero, queso quesadilla, or mozzarella cheese
2 poblano chilies

Roast poblano chilies in the flame of a gas stove, or under broiler in oven. The skin of the chile should be evenly blackened and blistered. Peel chili, remove stem and seeds, and slice into strips (see Basics).

In a small oven proof pan or casserole, place chile strips, then place cheese on top. Bake at 350° until cheese is melted and bubbling. Serve immediately with fresh tortillas.

Appetizer for 8 people

Salsa Chimichurri

1/3 cup peeled garlic cloves (about 25)
20 dried arbol chilies
1 1/2 cups cider vinegar
2 tsp. salt
1/4 cup parsley
3 cups olive oil (approximately)

Place garlic cloves, dried chilies, vinegar, salt and parsley in a blender container. Puree well. While blender is running, add olive oil in a very thin stream through feed hole into the vortex of the pureeing mixture. Continue to add oil until the vortex disappears. Store in the refrigerator.

Makes 4 1/2 cups

Arroz con Leche

(Rice Pudding)

6 cups whole milk
1 cup rice
2 sticks cinnamon
1 1/2 cups sugar
freshly ground cinnamon

Heat milk, rice and cinnamon sticks in a large saucepan. Bring milk to boil, and let simmer until rice is tender, stirring continuously, about 30 minutes. Add in sugar, and cook for another 5 minutes. Remove from heat.

Pudding will continue to thicken as it cools. Serve either warm or chilled, topped with freshly ground cinnamon.

Serves 8

Cabrito al Horno

Cabrito al Horno
(Baked Kid Goat)

Pico de Gallo con Aguacate
(Relish with Avocado)

Jamoncillo de Leche
(Milk Fudge)

I am shocked and amazed every time I hear that someone from our area either has never tried, or doesn't like *cabrito*. It is truly one of the delicacies of our area.

Cabrito can be stewed, baked, or roasted. But *Cabrito al Pastor* (Kid goat, shepherd style) can only be found in restaurants. The *cabritos* are extended on metal rods, and balanced in front of perfectly tended mesquite coals. Roasting *cabritos* in this fashion is such an art that the kitchens are focal points of the restaurants. The kitchen staff works behind large picture windows, so that you can inspect the entire process.

I would have to guess that goats helped conquer our rough and tough border terrain here, along with the Longhorn cattle. Settlers and immigrants needed animals that could take the tough environment and harsh conditions of South Texas ranch life. You can go to the most barren, God forsaken stretches of land in Mexico. The earth will be parched; the vegetation represented by sticks and dried up cactus. And there, coming around the bend, will be a little man with a herd of goats. Goats can survive anywhere.

The *jamoncillo* is a typical milk fudge candy that is served in the restaurants after a meal. *Jamoncillo* is also know as *leche quemada*, which means burnt milk. It will take you at least an hour to make this small batch of fudge, so get some extra cooks involved before you begin to make it. You need to constantly stir the milk, and scrape the bottom of the pan. Be careful, because you can burn this candy easily.

Serve with: rice, beans, corn tortillas, cold beer, margaritas

Cabrito al Horno
(Baked Kid Goat)

1 10 - 12 lb kid goat
salt, pepper, or your favorite seasoning mix

Heat your oven to 350°. Place goat in a large baking pan and season. (If carcass is too large, you may need to cut it in half and place in two ovens.) Place uncovered in oven for 1 1/2 to 2 hours. Serve warm.

You may want to take the meat out of the oven a little ahead of time and place on a hot grill to finish. This gives the meat a much better flavor and texture. Reserve the last 20-30 minutes of cooking time for the grill.

The goat head is considered a delicacy. If you wish to prepare the goat head, boil it whole for one hour, then add it to the baking pan for another 30-60 minutes.

Pico de Gallo con Aguacate

(Relish with Avocados)

2 avocados
1 tomato, seeded and chopped
1 cup onion, chopped
1/4 cup minced cilantro
salt to taste
1/4 cup minced serrano chilies (optional)

Cut avocado in half, removing the pit. Score the inside of the avocado horizontally and vertically. Scoop out the avocado into a bowl; it should come out neatly in cubes. Add in the remaining ingredients, toss lightly to mix, and salt to taste.

Makes 2 cups

Jamoncillo de Leche

(Milk Fudge)

1 3/4 cup sugar
1 quart milk
2 tsp. vanilla extract
1/2 cup chopped pecans

Place sugar and milk in a large heavy saucepan. Bring to a boil, and cook, stirring continuously, until you can see the bottom of the pan when you stir the candy. Make sure your mixture is stiff and well cooked, but not burned. Candy needs to be well cooked in order for it to harden properly. Cooking time is around 1 hour. Add vanilla extract to the candy at this point, and stir to combine well. Pour candy into a buttered 4"x 8" loaf pan. Press pecans onto top of candy while still hot. Allow to cool, then cut into pieces.

Makes 1 lb

Grilled Quail

Grilled Quail

Fresh Corn Bread

Orange Almond Salad

Vanilla Ice Cream
(purchased)

The corn bread recipe is from my aunt Mildred Chapa. I must have gotten this recipe from her when I was around 12 years old. She had a beautiful house in Cuernavaca, Morelos, Mexico, which is about an hour outside of Mexico City. She was a great cook, and a fine lady.

Her house, for me, will always be a collage of exotic, fanciful, and sometimes frightening images. She had french poodles that balanced themselves on the walls of the front entrance. For a long time, I thought they were statues. She had screaming peacocks, mango trees, and some very strange trees with peanut shaped pods hanging down, which must have weighed about 5 lbs each. Every breeze carried the aroma of guava and basil. For a kid, it was sensory overload.

Grilled Quail

- Marinade:
- 2 sticks margarine, melted
- 3 lemons or limes, cut in half
- 2 garlic cloves, minced
- 2 tsp. dry mustard
- 2 tsp. soy sauce
- 4 tbsp. Worcestershire sauce
- 4 tbsp. cider vinegar

- 8 quail
- lemon pepper seasoning

Combine marinade ingredients in a glass pan. Squeeze lemon or lime juice into mixture and leave in the spent lemon rind. Place quail in glass dish and let marinate for 3-4 hours, or overnight in fridge.

Season with lemon pepper seasoning and grill over open grill flame for 8 minutes on each side (may take longer for farm raised quail).

Serves 4

Fresh Corn Bread

3 ears of corn, kernels cut off
1 stick butter, softened
3 eggs
1 tsp. baking powder
1/2 of a 14oz can of condensed milk

Heat oven to 300°. Butter and flour a 9" glass pie plate. Place all of the ingredients in a blender container. Puree well. Pour into the prepared pie plate. Bake for one hour, or until golden brown and slightly firm.

Serves 8

Orange Almond Salad

- Mixed salad greens, about 3 cups
- 1/2 cup slivered blanched almonds
- 2 oranges, sectioned with membranes removed

Dressing:
- 2 tbsp. heavy cream
- 1/4 cup olive oil
- 1/4 tsp. sugar
- 1/4 tsp. dried dill
- pinch salt
- pinch pepper
- 1 green onion, finely chopped

2 tbsp. apple cider vinegar

Combine greens, orange sections and almonds in a salad bowl or on four salad plates. Except for the vinegar, whisk together all of the dressing ingredients. When homogenous, drizzle in the vinegar. Pour over salad right before serving.

Serves 4

Venison Henry

Venison Henry

Egg Noodles with Parmesan

Mock Caesar Salad

Ate con Queso

We cook a lot of venison here on the ranch. The Venison Henry is a dish that my husband and I have worked on for a while. The venison has to be cooked very quickly. Since venison has a low fat content, cooking it too long will make it tough. Several people have told me of venison they have stewed for hours, and it is fork tender, but this has never been my personal experience. I always cook venison for very short amounts of time, with the exception of venison chili, where the meat is ground.

Venison Henry

- 3 tbsp. butter
- 3/4 cup flour
- 1/2 cup grated parmesan cheese
- 1 1/2 lbs venison, thinly sliced

- Sauce:
- 3 tbsp. butter
- 1 cup sliced mushrooms
- 3 green onions, sliced
- 2 tbsp. chopped parsley
- 1 tbsp. cornstarch
- 1/2 cup beef broth
- 1/2 cup red or white wine
- salt and pepper

In a large skillet, melt butter. Meanwhile, combine flour and parmesan. Dredge venison in flour mixture, they fry in heated butter, 1 minute on each side. Drain cooked venison on paper towels, and keep warm.

In same skillet, melt remaining butter. Saute mushrooms, onions and parsley, until tender. Add cornstarch, and mix well. Add beef broth and wine, and continue to stir to combine ingredients until mixture thickens into a sauce. Salt and pepper to taste. Serve over cooked venison immediately.

Serves 4

Egg Noodles with Parmesan

1 12oz pkg egg noodles
2 tbsp. chopped parsley
2 tbsp. butter
1/3 cup grated parmesan cheese

Fill a large pot with water, and bring to boiling point. Add noodles, and cook according to package directions. When cooked, drain water, and rinse noodles well.

In same pot, melt butter with parsley. Remove from heat. Add parmesan and noodles, tossing to coat well.

Serves 4

Mock Caesar Salad

6 cloves garlic, minced
1 egg
1 cup olive oil
3 tbsp. whole grain mustard
1 tbsp. anchovy paste or 5 anchovy fillets
9 tbsp. red wine vinegar
mixed greens or Romaine lettuce, 1 handful
     per person

Blend first 5 ingredients together. Add vinegar slowly, whisking continuously. Make sure mixture is homogenous before serving. Serve over mixed greens. Two tablespoons of dressing equals one serving.

Makes 1 1/2 cups

Ate con Queso

Ate (pronounced AH-teh) is a "paste" made out of fruit. Actually, it is not what I would consider a "paste" at all, but a solid puree of fruit and sugar. Fruit jams or jellies are not to be substituted for this candy. There are several varieties, made out of apples, pears, guava, quince, and strawberries. My favorite is guava. Look for it in your grocer's ethnic food section, sometimes labeled as, for example, "guava paste", or whatever the flavor. Serve slices of the candy with your favorite sharp or mellow cheese. The salty cheese contrasts nicely with the sweet *ate*, and you'll find yourself unable to stop nibbling.

New Year's Eve

Puerco en Pipian
(Pork in Pumpkin Seed Sauce)

Black eyed Peas

Arroz con Platanos
(Rice with Plantains)

Buñuelos
(Tortilla Fritters)

Margaritas en las Rocas
(Margaritas on the Rocks)

New Year's Eve has been celebrated at my house since my husband and I married. Both sides of our family come over to ring in the New Year. In this menu, I have combined special Mexican dishes with the Southern tradition of pork and black eyed peas for the New Year's meal.

Inevitably, someone gets the brainy idea to shoot fireworks in my front yard. My dogs end up in the house, wrapping their shaking bodies around my ankles. The men are outside yukking it up, lighting firecrackers with their cigars, the women are fleeing the area, and I am tripping over dogs, cats and kids trying to get the meal to the buffet table. All the while drinking a very strong margarita.

Serve with: tortillas (Note: This is a great time to bring out some of those food gifts you received at Christmas.)

Puerco en Pipian

(Pork in Pumpkin Seed Sauce)

6 lbs pork loin

Sauce:
1/2 cup lard
1/2 lb raw unsalted pumpkin seeds
1/4 lb raw peanuts
1/2 cup sesame seeds
6 serrano chilies
1 onion, peeled and sliced
6 tomatillos, husked, washed, and boiled (or use canned)
3 cloves garlic
2 lettuce leaves
1/4 cup chopped cilantro
2 radishes, with tops
1 - 2 cups water
salt to taste

Heat 1-2 tablespoons of the lard in a skillet. Fry the pumpkin seeds, peanuts and sesame seeds for about 5 minutes. Remove skillet contents to a separate bowl, then add a bit more lard to the skillet. Fry the chilies, the onion, and tomatillos for about 5 minutes. Add garlic, and fry for another minute. Place the nut and seed mixture, and the fried chili mixture in a blender. Add in the lettuce leaves, cilantro, the radish leaves (reserve radish root for garnish) and enough water to facilitate blending. Puree mixture well. (If your blender seems overloaded, you may need to puree in batches.

Heat remaining lard in a fresh skillet. Add in pureed sauce. Simmer for 20 minutes, until slightly reduced. *(The sauce tastes better made one day in advance. If this is what you wish to do, then cool sauce and store in refrigerator or freezer until ready to use.)*

Trim excess fat from the pork, and cut into bite sized pieces. Place raw meat in a pot, cover with water, and boil until cooked, about 25-30 minutes.

Heat sauce in a large dutch oven, adding in some of the pork broth to thin sauce to desired thickness. Add in cooked pork, and allow to simmer 15 minutes before serving. Arrange radish slices on top of pipian before serving.

Serves 8

Black Eyed Peas

3 cups dried black eyed peas, picked over
1 onion, chopped
1 tomato, chopped
2 whole cloves garlic
2 tbsp. chopped cilantro
2 whole serrano chilies
3 slices chopped bacon or ham
salt to taste

Pick over peas, rinse well. Place in large pot and cover with water (at least five times the depth of the amount of dried peas.) Add onion, tomato, garlic, bacon or ham, cilantro, chilies and salt.

Bring to a boil, then lower heat to simmer until tender, about one hour. Let cool fully before storing in fridge.

Serves 8 - 12

Arroz con Platanos

(Rice with Plantains)

2 cups white long grained rice
2 - 3 tbsp. corn oil
1/4 onion, sliced
4 cups chicken broth or water
salt

2 plantains, very ripe
oil for frying (about 1/2 cup)

In a lidded skillet, heat oil. Add in rice and onion slices. Sauté until rice is opaque. Pour in chicken broth or water. When liquid returns to a boil, add salt and place lid on the skillet. Lower the flame to simmer, and cook over a low heat for 25 minutes. DO NOT LIFT LID!

Peel plantains, and slice diagonally into ovals, 1/4 inch thick. In a separate skillet, heat the oil for frying. Fry plantain slices until they are golden brown on each side. Drain on paper towels.

Place cooked rice in a serving dish. Garnish with cooked plantains.

Serves 8

Buñuelos
(Tortilla Fritters)

Follow the recipe for making flour tortillas (see Basics). Roll out tortillas, but do not cook tortillas on a griddle. Instead, heat about 2 cups of oil in a skillet. When the oil is hot, add in the raw tortilla. Fry for 60 seconds, until the tortilla becomes crispy. Turn over to other side. The tortilla should be blistered and golden. Drain on paper towels. Mix together 1 cup of sugar and two teaspoons ground cinnamon for every 10 *buñuelos* you make. While still hot, sprinkle cinnamon sugar on each side. Cool, and store in an airtight container. *Buñuelos* should keep for about 2 weeks.

Margaritas en las Rocas
(Margaritas on the Rocks)

3 cups of fine tequila
1 1/2 cups triple sec, or your favorite orange liquor
1/2 cup fresh lime juice
1 tbsp. sugar
2 limes, quartered
salt, poured onto a plate
olives on toothpicks, for garnish
plenty of cracked ice

Stir together the tequila, triple sec and lime juice. Add in sugar, and stir to dissolve.

Rub the rim of a medium sized cocktail glass with a lime slice. Dip glass rim into the salt to coat. Add ice and olive garnish. Pour margarita over the ice.

Serves 8 - 12

Fried Eggs with Mild Green Sauce

Fried Eggs with Mild Green Sauce

Fried Plantains

Atole de Fresa

This menu is designed for two people who want a nice meal, but don't want to cook and make a big production. This is a "let's stay at home tonight because its raining" comfort meal. In my household, we usually have all these ingredients on hand, except for maybe the strawberries.

Atole is a traditional beverage in Mexico. It is a cross between hot chocolate and pudding. You can make *atole* from the ground corn flour used to make corn tortillas, or from milk mixed with cornstarch.

Easy is the essence of this meal. So get out those fuzzy slippers and those old sweats from college, turn on a classic movie, and leave the dishes for in the morning.

Serve with: refried beans, tortillas, coffee

Fried Eggs with Mild Green Sauce

If you can fry an egg, skip this bit. If you can't, read on.

To fry an egg is very simple, but don't skimp on the oil, especially if you are not using a teflon pan. Heat about 1/2 cup of oil in a skillet. Crack your eggs, however many you'd like, in a separate dish, making sure the yolks don't break. When your oil is heated, add in your eggs. Baste the tops of the eggs with spoonfuls of hot oil. When they are cooked to your liking, then remove them from the pan, and place on a plate. Blot the oil off the top of the egg with a paper towel, if you like.

Teflon pans are the best for eggs. In my experience, cast iron and enamel coated cast iron are the worst. Teflon pans need the least amount of oil, and eggs tend to stick less.

Here's a trick you can only do with a teflon pan: Heat one tablespoon of oil in a teflon pan with a lid, coating the bottom of the pan well. Add your eggs, and allow the white of the egg to "set." When the whites are firm, add in one ounce of water, and top pan with lid. After a minute, your eggs are done. The water steams the egg, giving you a "fried" egg without the oil.

Mild Green Sauce

1 onion, sliced
1 1/2 lbs fresh tomatillos,
    or one 28oz can prepared whole tomatillos
1 clove garlic
2 whole serrano chilies (optional)
salt to taste

If using fresh tomatillos, husk and wash them, then place the tomatillos in a saucepan, covering them with water. Bring water to boil, and allow to simmer for about 10 minutes, or until tomatillos turn from bright green to a dull olive color. Drain water, and set aside.

If using canned tomatillos, drain water, then set aside.

Place tomatillos with garlic in a blender and puree. Set aside. In a clean skillet, fry the onion in a bit of oil. Add in tomatillo puree, and whole chilies. Salt to taste, and allow to simmer for 10 minutes, until slightly reduced.

Makes 2 cups

Fried Plantains

- If you are unfamiliar with plantains, you need to know that they are considered ripe when they are completely black. They shouldn't be moldy or too shriveled. They are not as soft as regular bananas, but they should not be so hard that they seem challenging to chew.

1 plantain per person
oil for frying, about 1 cup

Heat oil in a frying pan. Peel plantain, and slice in diagonal rounds, so they look like ovals from the top. Fry sliced bananas, turning once, until slightly browned on each side. Serve immediately.

Atole de Fresa

Try banana, pineapple, or mango *atole*, using the same proportions of fruit to milk as listed below.

1/2 cup fresh strawberries
2 cups milk
1/3 cup sugar
2 tbsp. cornstarch

Combine milk and strawberries in a blender. Puree well. Add sugar. Set aside 1/2 cup of milk mixture.

Pour strawberry milk mixture into a saucepan. Combine cornstarch with remaining 1/2 cup of milk mixture. When cornstarch is completely dissolved, add into saucepan. Heat and bring milk to simmering point, stirring constantly. Atole is ready to serve when hot and thickened. Sprinkle with ground nutmeg and cinnamon, if desired.

Serves 2

Tortilla Soup

Tortilla Soup
Coconut and Vanilla Bean Pudding

Tortilla Soup is a great "help yourself" sort of meal. Everyone jazzes up their soup the way they want it. I love to make this for guests. You should make it a day before serving it so that the flavors have time to mature. It is also a good opportunity to use that soup tureen that you have stashed away.

Take the time to make the Coconut and Vanilla Bean Pudding. Your guests will love it.

Tortilla Soup

- Soup:
- 2 pasilla chilies
- 2 ancho chilies
- 4 tomatoes (or 6 roma tomatoes), chopped
- 1 onion, chopped
- 4 cloves garlic, peeled
- 4 quarts defatted chicken broth
- salt
- 1 tbsp. chopped cilantro

- Toppings (prepare in advance):
- 12 - 20 tortillas, cut into thin strips
- Oil

- 1 6 oz pkg Queso Fresco or Feta cheese, crumbled
- 3 - 4 avocados, sliced
- 1/2 head iceberg lettuce, shredded
- 1 cup mexican sour cream, or 1 cup regular sour cream, thinned with a little milk
- 1 onion, finely chopped

In a small saucepan, boil chilies until they are softened. When soft and cool, remove stem, seeds, and veins. Place chilies in a blender container, along with tomatoes, onion, garlic, and about 1 cup of chicken broth (enough to facilitate blending). Puree well.

In a large stock pot, heat remaining chicken broth, and add in chile puree. Salt to taste, and add cilantro. Simmer for about 30 minutes. *(Tastes better made one day in advance.)*

Fry tortilla strips in oil, until crispy. Serve soup in individual bowls, or in a large tureen. Serve all toppings and tortilla strips in separate dishes, so that each person can garnish their soup to their liking.

Serves 8

Note: *You can bake the tortilla strips in the oven, and avoid the frying altogether, although the texture is a bit tougher. Without the fried tortillas and the rich toppings, this is a great low-fat meal.*

Coconut and Vanilla Bean Pudding

4 cups milk
1 fresh coconut, shelled and peeled, and cut in small chunks
1 cup sugar
1/2 tsp. salt
1/4 cup cornstarch
1 vanilla bean
2 eggs, well beaten
2 tbsp. unsalted butter

In a blender container, add 2 cups of milk and the coconut. Blend until you have a very smooth liquid. Add more of the remaining milk if necessary for smooth blending.

In a large saucepan, combine the blended coconut milk mixture, sugar, salt and corn-starch. Add any remaining milk. Break vanilla bean, and add into pot. Cook mixture over medium heat until mixture starts to gently boil. Cook for two more minutes. Remove from heat.

Whisking eggs continuously, add in about a cup of the hot pudding into the eggs, one spoonful at a time. Add egg mixture back into remaining pudding. Add butter and stir well. Cool to room temperature, then chill before serving.

Serves 8

Note: *Freshly grated coconut is a tough order, but worth the effort. Select a coconut that sounds like it has plenty of milk when you shake it. Puncture one of the eyes of the coconut (one out of the three "eyes" is easy to puncture, so try them all), and drain the milk into a glass. Heat oven to 325°, and bake whole coconut for 1 hour. Remove from oven, and let cool. Crack shell, and coconut meat should separate easily from shell. Peel off brown husk with a sharp knife, cutting away from you. Vegetable peelers work well too, but you may get a blister on your thumb. Grate coconut in your food processor or use as directed above. Then, take a nap.*

Chicken Fried Steak

Chicken Fried Steak with Cream Gravy

Mashed Potatoes

Drop Bisquits
with Strawberry Lime Jam

Chocolate Pie

If any of my mother's children had to choose a last meal, this would be it.

When I went up East to college, I would talk with my friends about our favorite home foods. None of them could figure out why it was called "Chicken Fried Steak" if there was no chicken in it. Yankees are always so literal. I guess its proper title should be "Steak cooked in the style of Fried Chicken." But this would confuse them as well. I made it a few times for my friends. Then, they saw the light. The term is now permanently part of their lexicon.

Chicken Fried Steak With Cream Gravy

Steak:
3 lbs beef round steak
shortening or oil for frying
3 - 4 eggs
1/4 cup milk
1 cup all purpose flour
salt and pepper

Gravy:
4 cups milk
1/3 cup all purpose flour
salt to taste
freshly cracked black pepper

Trim fat from steak, and cut into portion size steaks, about 3"x 4". With a meat tenderizing hammer, pound the steaks well on both sides. Heat shortening or oil in a large skillet.

In a deep dish, beat eggs well and add 1/4 cup milk. In another deep dish, add flour, and season with salt and pepper. Dip a steak in the egg mixture, then dredge in the seasoned flour. Place steak in the hot oil. Prepare remaining steaks in the same manner, accommodating as many pieces as possible in the frying pan.

When the accumulated juices on the top of each steak turns dark red, turn then steak over to brown on the other side, about 5 minutes on each side. Make sure coating is well browned. When steak is cooked, remove from pan and drain on paper toweling. Continue to cook remaining steaks. Cooked steaks can be held in a warm oven.

Drain all but 3 tablespoons of drippings from the pan. Leave any browned bits of coating that may have accumulated, scraping the bottom of the pan gently to loosen them. Return pan to heat. Add in 1/3 cup of flour, utilizing any dredging flour that may be left over, adding in fresh flour, if needed. Continue to scrape up brown bits with spoon, while mixing flour with the drippings. Once your "roux" is well combined, add in 4 cups of milk. Simmer gravy until it starts to thicken, about 10-15 minutes. Salt and pepper to taste.

Serve steaks with gravy immediately.

Serves 6

Mashed Potatoes

4 lbs russet potatoes, peeled and cut into chunks
1 cup heavy cream
4 tbsp. butter
salt to taste

Place potatoes in a large pot, and cover with water. Boil potatoes until they are easily pierced in the center with a fork. Drain water.

Add in cream and butter, and mash potatoes well with a potato masher, or whip with an electric mixer. Salt to taste.

Serves 6

rop Biscuits

2 cups flour
1 tbsp. baking powder
1/3 cup shortening
1 cup milk
1 tbsp. sugar

Heat oven to 450°. Mix together flour, baking powder and shortening, until mixture resembles coarse meal. Add in milk and sugar, and stir well until you have a soft dough. Drop in rounded spoonfuls onto an ungreased cookie sheet. Bake for 15 minutes, or until golden brown.

Makes 10 - 12 biscuits

trawberry Lime Jam

- 4 lbs strawberries, washed and hulled
- 2 tbsp. lime juice
- 1 tbsp. grated lime peel
- 7 cups sugar
- 1 pkg powdered pectin

Place all ingredients in stainless steel or non-reactive kettle. Turn stove to medium heat and begin to cook jam mixture. As strawberries cook, mash them with potato masher. Bring jam to boil, and let simmer 40 minutes. Stir often and skim foam from top.

Ladle hot jam into warm canning jars. Secure lids and process in a water bath according to directions on pectin packet.

Makes nine 8 oz jars, plus a "taster"

Chocolate Pie

1 pre-baked 9" pie shell (see Basics)

Filling:
1 1/4 cups sugar
1/4 cup cornstarch
pinch salt
3 cups milk
2 oz unsweetened chocolate
4 eggs, separated
2 tbsp. butter
2 tsp. vanilla

Meringue:
2 egg whites, plus the 4 egg whites previously reserved
pinch salt
6 tbsp. sugar

Combine sugar, cornstarch, salt, milk and chocolate in a saucepan. Heat, stirring constantly, until mixture thickens, and appears to have a smooth chocolate color. Remove from heat.

In a separate bowl, beat egg yolks with an electric hand mixer. Add in hot chocolate mixture one spoonful at a time while still using the hand mixer, until you have added in about 1 cup. Turn off hand mixer, then add egg mixture back into saucepan. Cook for another two minutes, stirring to combine well. Add in butter and vanilla. When butter is completely melted, pour chocolate mixture into prepared pie shell. Chill until firm.

Heat oven to 350°. Whip egg whites and salt in mixer at top speed until frothy, then add in sugar, one spoonful at a time. When the egg whites are very stiff, pour on top of chocolate pie, sealing edges. Bake in oven for about 12 minutes, until the meringue is golden.

Serves 8

Guisado de Pollo

Guisado de Pollo
(Chicken Stew)

Guacamole

Pastel Tres Leches
(Three Milk Cake)

This dish in English would be called "Chicken Stew", but much is lost in the translation. This *guisado* is tangy and light, but still a nice comfort food. And, for those dieting, it is very low in fat. In fact, you can cut the oil in the sauce down to a mist of vegetable spray so nothing sticks to your cooking pan. Also, rub the cooked chicken between your fingers so that you get a finely shredded chicken.

The *Pastel Tres Leches* is a very trendy cake in Mexico. The milk poured over the cake will gather in the bottom of the pan, but that is the nature of the beast. You can drain off some of the milk, invert the milk soaked cake on a platter, and frost it for a better presentation, but I recommend leaving it in the pan and serving it on individual plates in the kitchen.

Serve with: tortillas, rice and beans

Guisado de Pollo
(Chicken Stew)

Chicken:
1 whole chicken, about 3 lbs
1 onion, quartered
1 - 2 tomatoes, quartered
2 whole serrano chilies
2 cloves garlic, peeled
salt to taste

Sauce:
water
1 lb fresh tomatoes, or one 14oz can whole tomatoes
1 onion, finely chopped
2 tbsp. oil
2 cloves garlic
pinch ground comino
2 serrano chilies
salt

Boil chicken with onion, tomatoes, chilies, garlic and salt. Remove chicken from broth; reserve broth for another meal.

When chicken is cool, separate the meat from the bones and skin. Discard bones and skin. Shred chicken finely by rubbing pieces between fingers to separate fibers. Set aside.

For the sauce, combine garlic and tomatoes in a blender. Add just enough water to facilitate blending, then puree.

In a skillet, add oil, and saute onions, until translucent. Add pureed tomatoes, comino and chilies, and allow to simmer of about 5 minutes. Add chicken, and simmer for 20 minutes, or until liquid is reduced. Salt to taste.

Serves 6

Guacamole

- **4 ripe avocados**
- **1 tbsp. minced cilantro (optional)**
- **juice of 1 lemon**
- **1/2 cup chopped tomatoes**
- **1/2 cup chopped onion**
- **salt to taste**

Cut avocados in half, removing and reserving pits. On a plate, mash avocados with a fork. When smooth, add in remaining ingredients, folding in with fork. Spoon into a serving dish. Use the pits as a garnish, as they prevent the guacamole from turning brown.

Makes about 2 cups

Pastel Tres Leches

(Three Milk Cake)

Cake:
7 eggs, separated
1/2 cup butter, softened
1 cup sugar
2 1/2 cups flour
1 tsp. baking powder
1/2 tsp. salt
1 cup milk
1 tsp. vanilla

Milks:
1 12oz can evaporated milk
1 14oz can condensed milk
1 cup heavy cream

Frosting:
6 egg whites
1 cup sugar
1 cup corn syrup
juice of 1/2 lemon

Lemon or lime zest

Grease and flour a 9"x13" baking pan. Heat the oven to 350°. In a bowl, cream together the egg yolks, butter, and sugar. In a separate bowl, combine the flour, baking powder, and salt. Add flour mixture alternately with the 1 cup of milk to the egg mixture. Add in vanilla. Beat egg whites until stiff. Fold into cake batter, then pour into prepared pan. Bake for 25-30 minutes, until a toothpick comes clean out of the center. Cool cake in pan on a cake rack.

Combine evaporated milk, condensed milk and cream. Pour over the cake. Allow cake to absorb the milk for about 2 hours.

To prepare frosting: Boil water in the bottom of a double boiler. In the top of the double boiler, combine the egg whites and sugar. Beat the egg whites until stiff. In a very thin stream, pour in the corn syrup. Add lemon juice. Frosting should be thick and shiny. Spread over top of cake. Garnish with lemon or lime zest. When you serve the cake, the milks should collect in the bottom of the pan.

Serves 16

Fried Oysters

Fried Oysters with Tomato-Chipotle Sauce

Buttermilk Coleslaw

Lemon Meringue Pie

This menu was inspired by my grandfather. He loves oysters, and dreams about lemon pies. I do know that since cabbage is a green vegetable, he would skip the coleslaw. More for me.

Serve with: baked or fried potatoes

Fried Oysters with Tomato-Chipotle Sauce

Sauce:

2 dried chipotle chilies

2 fresh red roma tomatoes,
      or one large regular tomato, chopped

2 cloves garlic, peeled

1/2 large onion, roughly chopped

1 tbsp. dijon mustard

1/4 cup water

salt to taste

1 tbsp. olive oil

Boil chipotle chilies in water until they are softened. Remove stem, and place in a blender container. Add in tomatoes, garlic, onion, mustard and water. Blend until well combined. Add more water if the blender cannot function properly. Salt to taste.

In a small skillet, heat oil. When oil is hot, add in sauce puree, and simmer. Allow sauce to reduce, about 20 minutes, stirring occasionally. The sauce can be served either warm or cold with the Fried Oysters.

Oysters:
1 quart raw oysters, shucked
shortening or oil for deep frying
1 cup yellow cornmeal
1 cup all purpose flour
2 cups regular milk or buttermilk
1 egg

Heat cooking oil or shortening in a large skillet. On a sheet of waxed paper or a plate, combine flour and cornmeal. In a separate bowl, whisk together milk and egg, combining well. Dip oysters in milk mixture, then dredge in flour mixture. Make sure oil is hot enough so that oyster starts to fry immediately. Fry each oyster for two minutes on one side, flip, then fry on other side for two minutes. Remove from oil, then drain oysters on paper toweling. Serve immediately with the Tomato-Chipotle sauce on the side.

Serves 4

Buttermilk Coleslaw

Dressing:
1/2 cup buttermilk
1/2 cup mayonnaise
1 cup sour cream
1 tbsp. sugar
2 tbsp. grated onion
1 tsp. celery seed
2 tbsp. lemon or lime juice
3 tbsp. apple cider vinegar
1/2 tsp. salt
freshly cracked black pepper, to taste

1 head cabbage, about 2 lbs
3 carrots, about 1/2 lb

Combine ingredients for dressing, and store in refrigerator until ready for use.

Shred cabbage and grate carrots. Toss cabbage and carrots with dressing right before serving.

Serves 8

Lemon Pie

1 pre-baked 9" pie shell (see Basics)

Filling:
2 cups sugar
3/4 cup flour
2 tbsp. cornstarch
1/2 tsp. salt
3 cups water
4 eggs, separated
1/2 cup lemon juice
2 tbsp. grated lemon rind

Meringue:
2 egg whites, plus the 4 egg whites previously reserved
pinch salt
12 tbsp. sugar

In a large saucepan, add sugar, flour, cornstarch, salt and water. Stir over medium flame until thickened and bubbling. Beat egg yolks with an electric hand mixer until lemon colored. While beating, add in one cup of hot cornstarch mixture, one spoonful at a time. Return egg yolk mixture to pot. Stir in lemon juice and lemon rind. Cool the mixture completely.

Fill pie shell with lemon filling. Heat oven to 350°.

For the meringue, add together the four remaining egg whites with the two extra egg whites. Add the pinch salt, and beat with and electric mixer until frothy. Start to add in sugar, one tablespoon at a time. Beat meringue until stiff peaks form. Mound meringue over the filled pie, sealing edges. Bake for 12-15 minutes until the meringue is golden. Cool, then serve.

Serves 8

Caldo de Mariscos

Caldo de Mariscos
(Seafood Soup)

Tostadas con Chile
(Toasted Tortillas with Chile)

Strawberry Pie

This menu has quite the dramatic presentation; whole crabs bobbing in the depths of a mysterious broth, fresh herbs floating on the surface, and a subtle fragrance. Surprisingly enough, it only takes about an hour to prepare this one-tureen dinner for eight. Don't forget the nut-crackers and seafood forks to get at the crab meat. And, as usual, this soup tastes even better the next day.

Caldo de Mariscos

(Seafood Soup)

- Water
- 2 serrano chilies, whole
- 1 whole head of garlic, unpeeled with loose husks removed
- 3 sprigs fresh oregano
- 3 sprigs fresh thyme
- 3 sprigs fresh marjoram
- 2 tbsp. chopped fresh cilantro
- 1 fish head (optional)
- 1 lb scallops
- 1 lb crab in shell, cut in half lengthwise (I use small blue crab, about 4oz apiece)
- 1 lb small shrimp, in shell
- 1 lb red snapper, or your favorite fish, cut in 1 inch pieces
- 1 lb of one or a combination of the following: squid, mussels, octopus, oysters
- 2 ancho chilies
- 1 lb tomatoes
- 1 onion, sliced
- 2 tbsp. oil
- salt to taste

Bring 5 quarts of water in a large stock pot to a boil. Add in chilies, garlic, oregano, thyme, marjoram, cilantro and fish head. Let boil for about 10 minutes. Add in crab and shrimp, continue to boil for 20 minutes. When the shrimp are cooked, remove as many as possible, and peel and devein them. Return shrimp to pot, and add remaining seafood. Lower heat to a simmer, and cook for 10 more minutes.

Meanwhile, boil the ancho chilies in about 2 cups of water, until chilies are soft. Drain and discard water. Remove seeds and stems, adding a few seeds back in for a spicier soup. In a blender container, add tomatoes, onions, cooked chiles, seeds and enough water to facilitate blending. Puree well. In a skillet, heat the oil. Pour in the pureed sauce, and simmer for about 10 minutes, until reduced and slightly thickened.

Add salt to taste. Add sauce to soup pot and combine well. Remove fish head. Serve hot.

Serves 8

Note: *I found a very convenient frozen seafood mixture that has a mixture of octopus, squid, mussels, shrimp, and other assorted shellfish. It came in a one pound bag, and was perfect for the one pound of mixed seafood that you need to complete this recipe.*

ostadas con Chile

(Toasted Tortillas with Chile)

16 - 24 corn tortillas
chile powder
salt

Heat your oven to 350°. Cut tortillas in quarters and place in a baking pan. Sprinkle chile and salt on tortillas, and bake, with oven door ajar, until the tortillas are crispy and slightly brown. Allow to cool on a cookie rack.

Serves 8

trawberry Pie

- 9" pre-baked pie shell (see Basics)
-
- Filling:
- 2 lbs fresh strawberries, about 6 cups
- 1 cup water
- 1/3 cup cornstarch
- 3/4 cup sugar
  juice of 1/2 lemon
-
- Whipped cream
- lime zest

Wash and hull the strawberries, setting aside one cup of the fruit. Place the one cup of berries in a saucepan with 1 cup of water. Boil the fruit for a few minutes, until soft. Mash cooked fruit with a potato masher. Pour liquid through a strainer, reserving the liquid. Discard the fruit, and cool strawberry juice completely. Return the cooled liquid to the saucepan. Sift in the cornstarch. Cook over a low flame until the mixture is clear and thick. Remove from heat. Add in sugar and lemon juice. Cool completely.

Pour 1/3 cup of the cooled glaze over the bottom of the pie shell. Arrange remaining fresh strawberries in the pie shell, slicing larger berries to make bite-sized. Pour remaining strawberry glaze over the top. Chill until ready to serve. Serve garnished with whipped cream and lime zest.

Serves 6 - 8

Curried Shrimp and Artichoke Shortcake

Curried Shrimp and Artichoke Shortcake

Sweet Potato Biscuits

Black Eyed Pea Salad

Pecan Tassies

Ladies in the South are forever having luncheons, bridge parties, teas, etc... and, bless me, if chicken salad doesn't make its appearance at every single one of these functions.

I think this menu is a nice alternative.

Serve with: coffee, tea, punch or champagne

Curried Shrimp and Artichoke Shortcake

- 2 tbsp. butter
- 2 tbsp. flour
- 2 cups half and half
- 1/4 tsp. curry powder
- 1/2 tsp. salt
  pinch cayenne pepper
- 2 tbsp. grated onion
- 2 tbsp. dry sherry or vermouth
- 2 lbs cooked shrimp, peeled and deveined
- 1 14oz can quartered artichoke hearts, drained

Melt butter in a skillet. Add flour, and incorporate all the butter. When well combined, add half and half, curry powder, salt, cayenne, and onion. Simmer sauce for about 10 minutes, stirring constantly. When sauce is thickened, add shrimp, artichokes, and sherry or vermouth, and simmer for 5 more minutes. Serve immediately over Sweet Potato Biscuits.

Serves 4

Sweet Potato Biscuits

2 cups all purpose flour
1 tsp. baking soda
1/2 tsp. salt
1 tbsp. sugar
1/4 cup shortening
1/2 cup cooked mashed sweet potato
3/4 cup buttermilk

Heat oven to 450°. In a large mixing bowl, combine flour, soda, salt and sugar. Add in shortening and sweet potato, mixing with hands until mixture resembles coarse meal. Add in buttermilk, just enough to form a cohesive dough that is not too soft. *(If you overdo the buttermilk, just try to knead in a little extra flour in the next step.)*

On a floured surface, knead the dough about 10 times. Roll out to 1/2 inch thickness, and cut with a biscuit cutter or a glass, about 2 1/2 inches in diameter. Bake on an ungreased cookie sheet for 10 - 12 minutes.

Makes 12 biscuits

Black Eyed Pea Salad

- 1 1/2 lbs fresh, shelled black eyed peas
- water
- 1 red bell pepper, stem and seeds removed, and finely chopped
- 1 red onion, peeled and finely chopped
- 1 16oz jar pickled sweet Hungarian wax peppers, drained, stemmed and sliced
- 3/4 cup olive oil
- 1/3 cup apple cider vinegar
- cracked pepper
- salt

Place black eyed peas in a saucepan, and cover with water. Bring to a boil, and simmer gently for 18-20 minutes. Drain water, and cool completely.

In a large mixing bowl, combine the bell pepper, onion, and wax peppers. Add in cooked black eyed peas. In a separate bowl, combine olive oil, vinegar, pepper, and salt, whisking to mix well. Pour over vegetables in mixing bowl, and toss gently, so as not to break peas. Chill and serve.

Serves 8 generously

Note: *I do not recommend dried black eyed peas for this salad, as they tend to be a little mushy when cooked.*

Pecan Tassies

Pastry:
3 oz cream cheese, softened
1/2 cup butter, softened
1 cup flour

Filling:
1 egg, beaten
3/4 cup brown sugar
1 tsp. vanilla
pinch salt
1 cup chopped pecans

With an electric mixer, combine the pastry ingredients until you have a soft dough. Chill the dough for one hour.

Heat oven to 325°. Divide dough into 24 portions. Roll into balls, then press balls into mini muffin pans (2 inches diameter). Use a little flour on your fingers if the dough gets sticky.

Whisk together the egg, brown sugar, vanilla and salt. Stir in the pecans. Pour the filling into the prepared pastries. Bake for 20-25 minutes.

Makes 24 pastries

Quesadillas

Quesadillas

Salsa de Chile de Arbol

Grilled Nopalitos and Tomato Salad

Trolebus de Papaya
(Papaya Slush)

In recent years, the *quesadilla* has been popping up on trendy restaurant menus across the country. It has been raised to height never before seen by a lowly comfort food. But mind you, I mean no disrespect. *Quesadillas* are the mainstay of many a childhood. It is a Mexican grilled cheese sandwich. They are eaten morning, noon, and night, and as snacks. They are grabbed on the way out the door, taken in the car, out to play, and to the sick in bed. They are quick to make and filling. Your kids will love them, and you'll be making an extra few for yourself.

Serve with: refried beans

Quesadillas

- 2 - 3 tortillas per person, either flour or corn
- cheese, preferably a Mexican asadero cheese, queso quesadilla, or Monterrey Jack

Heat tortillas on a griddle. Place a small slice of cheese on the heated tortilla, then fold tortilla in half over cheese to form a half circle. Let cheese melt, and tortilla toast. Serve immediately with *Salsa de Chile de Arbol*.

Note: *You can add in different things to your quesadilla: A slice of tomato, cilantro or a leaf of epazote, a little ham or cooked shrimp. Use your imagination.*

Serve with: Salsa de Chile de Arbol

Salsa de Chile de Arbol

(Very Hot!)

20 dried arbol chilies
2 cloves garlic, peeled
water
2 tbsp. oil
salt

Heat your oven to 350°. Place chilies on a baking sheet. Toast the chilies in the oven for 1 - 2 minutes. Be vigilant, as the chilies will burn quickly. Cool chilies.

Remove stems from chilies. Place chilies in the container of a blender with the cloves of garlic. Add in just enough water to facilitate blending. Puree well.

In a small skillet, heat oil. Add in chili puree, and saute until most of the water has evaporated out of the sauce. Salt to taste.

Makes about 1/2 cup

Grilled Nopalito and Tomato Salad

8 whole cactus leaves, washed and thorns removed
3 large ripe tomatoes (or 5 small), sliced in rounds
6 oz queso fresco or Feta cheese, crumbled

Dressing:
1/2 cup red wine vinegar
3/4 cup olive oil
2 cloves garlic, minced
2 sprigs fresh oregano
salt and freshly cracked pepper

Grill cactus leaves on a barbecue grill, until they change color from brilliant green to olive drab. Do not let burn or dry out. When cooked, cut into strips and set aside.

Combine dressing ingredients. Remove oregano leaves from stem. Use leaves in dressing, and discard the stem.

Arrange cactus and tomatoes on a plate. Sprinkle crumbled cheese over the top. Right before serving, pour dressing over salad.

Serves 6

Trolebus de Papaya

(Papaya Slush)

4 cups fresh papaya, peeled and chopped (discard seeds)
2 cups ice
water
1/4 cup sugar, or to taste

Place papaya, ice and sugar in a blender.
Begin to puree. Add in enough water to
facilitate blending. Puree until smooth.
Serve immediately.

Serves 4 - 6

Grilled Shrimp

Grilled Shrimp
with Tequila Garlic Marinade

Crunchy Skinned Baked Potatoes
with Pico de Gallo

Blueberry Crumble
with Skinny Cream

My sister Elizabeth is gorgeous. Knock-you-on-your-sitting-place gorgeous. It would be nice to have her looks. People always tell me how much they admire her, not only because she is so beautiful, but because she is such a nice person as well. I'm a nice person too. In fact, sometimes people tell me I'm smart... and a nice person. Sometimes people tell me I'm smart, witty... and a nice person. Noticing a pattern here? Ouch.

Anyway, this menu is dedicated to "Leevy", who is always on a diet.

Grilled Shrimp with Tequila Garlic Marinade

2 lbs large shrimp, peeled and deveined

1 cup tequila
1 onion, peeled and chopped
2 dried arbol chilies, stems removed
5 cloves garlic, peeled
1 tsp. salt
1/2 cup olive oil
1/2 cup cilantro

Skewer shrimp on bamboo skewers. Place in non-reactive dish and set aside.

Combine tequila, onion, chile, garlic, and salt in a blender container. Puree well, then slowly drizzle oil through top feed hole. At the last minute, add in cilantro and turn off blender. Pour over prepared shrimp. Marinate in the refrigerator for 30 minutes.

Remove skewered shrimp from marinade, and place on heated grill. Grill over a medium flame, about 5 minutes on each side, or until shrimp are no longer translucent. Baste with remaining marinade.

Serves 4

Crunchy Skinned Baked Potatoes with Pico de Gallo

Even though the microwave is great for speeding any cooking process, baked potatoes come out unevenly cooked, raw in some places, and never crunchy. I personally find them lacking in good 'tater flavor as well. Use a conventional oven for this recipe.

4 large baking potatoes, such as Russets
vegetable oil
salt

Heat your oven to 450°. Scrub your potatoes under running water with a vegetable brush. Prick holes in the skin with a fork, then rub with the vegetable oil. Place the potatoes in a baking pan, and sprinkle them with salt. Place in the oven for 1 hour.

Pico de Gallo

A small food processor or mini chopper is ideal for making a quick batch of Pico de Gallo. This also makes a great "salsa" for chips.

1 onion, finely chopped
2 tomatoes, seeded, and finely chopped
1/2 cup cilantro, finely chopped
6 serrano chilies, finely chopped
salt

Combine ingredients and salt to taste. Serve over baked potatoes. Can be made in advance and stored in the refrigerator.

Serves 4

Blueberry Crumble with Skinny Cream

1 cup graham cracker crumbs
2 tbsp. water
1 1/2 tsp. melted margarine
1/4 tsp. cinnamon
2 tbsp. cornstarch
1/4 cup sugar
2 1/2 cups frozen blueberries
1 cup skim milk, well chilled

Preheat oven to 350°. Combine crumbs, water, melted margarine and cinnamon. Mix well and set aside.

In separate bowl, combine sugar and cornstarch. Add blueberries and combine well.

Divide blueberry mixture into eight custard dishes. Sprinkle equal portions of the graham cracker mixture on the top of the blueberries. Bake for 20 minutes.

Right before you are ready to serve your blueberry crumbles, place the skim milk in the bowl of a food processor. Add sugar, then start food processor. Milk will become frothy and stiff, like whipped cream, without the fat. Serve immediately with your blueberry crumble, as this illusion does not last long!

Serves 8

Shrimp Boil

Shrimp Boil

Homemade Red Sauce

Lime Ice Box Pie

My grandfather Willis taught me how to make this shrimp boil when I was fairly young. I was amazed that he didn't have to go to the store to buy one of those little muslin bags with the properly measured and combined spices. Really, to me, this is much easier, and more fun, because the spices end up all over the shrimp shells. It makes a pretty picture when you sit down to peel them.

I suggest you spread out some newspaper, and have your guests get down and dirty with your shrimp boil. You could even add in a few blue crabs to the boil, and make your guests really work.

The pie is an easy do ahead dessert. Buy a few baguettes, some nice beer, and you have the makings for a memorable evening.

Serve with: French bread, ice cold beer

Shrimp Boil

- 5 lbs large shrimp
- 3 limes, cut in half
- 1 tbsp. peppercorns
- 3 tbsp. coriander seeds
- 3 dried red chilies, preferably chile de arbol
- 3 cloves garlic, peeled
- 2 bay leaves
- 1 tbsp. mustard seeds

Fill a large pot with water, and bring to a boil. Add in the limes and spices while the water heats. When the water is at a full rolling boil, add the shrimp, return to a boil and cook for 5 minutes, until the shrimp are pink and the shell separates from the back. Drain water, and pack hot shrimp in ice to cool.

Serves 4

Homemade Red Sauce

(Homemade Ketchup)

Cheesecloth

Spices:
1/2 tsp. whole mustard seed
1/2 tsp. whole allspice berries
1/2 tsp. whole peppercorns
1/2 tsp. whole coriander seeds
2 cloves (whole)
pinch celery seed
2 tbsp. brown sugar
1/2 stick cinnamon
1 bay leaf

1 28oz can whole peeled tomatoes (do not drain)
1 onion, chopped
1/4 bell pepper, chopped
1 rib celery with leaves, chopped
1 clove garlic, minced
1 whole serrano or jalapeño chili
1/2 cup vinegar

To make the spice sachet: Cut a double layer of cheesecloth into a 5" inch square. In the center of the square, place mustard seeds, allspice berries, peppercorns, coriander seeds, cloves and celery seeds. Tie corners of cloth together to make a bundle. Set aside.

- Puree the tomatoes, onion, bell pepper, celery, garlic, chili and vinegar together in a blender. Place puree in a skillet, and add spice sachet, brown sugar, cinnamon, and bay leaf. Simmer for 30 minutes, until the sauce is reduced. Cool slightly, then store sauce in the refrigerator with the spices for 1-2 weeks.

- Remove sauce from refrigerator. Remove spice sachet, cinnamon and bay leaf. Add in desired amount of prepared horseradish to make a red sauce (about 2-3 tablespoons), and serve.

Prepared Horseradish

- 1 fresh horseradish root, washed, peeled, and chopped
  1/2 - 1 cup white vinegar

- Place chopped fresh horseradish in the container of a blender. Add in barely enough vinegar to puree the horseradish. You do not want the flavor of the horseradish to be overpowered by the vinegar. Puree until very smooth, inspecting it closely to remove any large pieces.

- This will freeze well for future use. Since only a few tablespoons at a time are needed, you may want to freeze the puree in ice cube trays, and store the frozen horseradish blocks in a plastic container.

Lime Icebox Pie

Crust:
7 1/2 sheets graham crackers, broken (4 crackers per sheet)
6 tbsp. butter
1/4 cup sugar

Filling:
2 eggs, separated
1 14oz can condensed milk
1/2 cup lime juice
1 tbsp. grated lime peel
1/4 tsp. vanilla
1/2 cup sugar
2 drops green food color (optional)

Heat oven to 350°. Grind crackers, butter and sugar until very fine in a food processor. You need about 2 cups of this crumb mixture to make a pie-crust. Press crumbs into a 9" glass pie plate. Bake for 10-12 minutes. Remove from oven and allow to cool.

Whisk together egg yolks and condensed milk. When well mixed, add in lime juice, lime peel, vanilla, sugar and food coloring.

In a separate bowl, beat egg whites until stiff. Fold into condensed milk mixture, and pour into pie crust. Freeze pie until firm, at least two hours before serving.

Serves 8

Beef Tenderloin

Beef Tenderloin

Pasta with Sundried Tomato
and Spinach Pesto

Broccoli with Breadcrumbs

Flan de Cafe
(Coffee Caramel Custard)

My sister Mary Margaret serves this menu whenever she has guests. She said the tenderloin should be at room temperature to fully enjoy its flavor. I agree, plus it makes it easier if you're not rushing around to get a piping hot meal on the table when your guests arrive.

For me, the quintessential beef tenderloin is rare in the center, without being raw, and well browned and flavorful on the outside. Cooking tenderloin is a snap. Calculate 4 1/2 minutes per pound for the perfectly rare tenderloin. That means 18 minutes in a very hot oven for a 4 lb tenderloin. Add in one more minute per pound for medium doneness.

Mary Margaret is really into flan as well, so I added a coffee flan. This recipe is different from the Orange Flan found elsewhere in this book, in that it calls for condensed milk. The condensed milk gives the custard a more dense, rich texture. You can leave out the instant coffee if you want a plain flan. Mary Margaret would.

Beef Tenderloin

- 1 beef tenderloin, about 4 lbs

- Marinade:
  1/2 onion, minced
  1 cup olive oil
  1/3 cup red wine vinegar
  1 heaping tbsp. dijon mustard
  3 cloves garlic, minced
  salt and pepper

Combine marinade ingredients in a bowl. Place uncooked tenderloin in a glass baking dish. Pour marinade over. Cover with plastic, and allow meat to marinate for at least 4 hours.

Heat oven to 475°. Remove tenderloin from the glass baking dish and place in a baking pan. Discard marinade. Bake the tenderloin for the amount of time you have calculated, or test with a meat thermometer to see if the meat has reached your desired degree of doneness. Remove from oven, and allow to cool before serving.

Serves 8

Pasta with Sundried Tomato and Spinach Pesto

1 lb dried pasta (raddiatore, gemelli, spirals,
    orzo, or your favorite shape)

Pesto:
2 oz fresh spinach, well washed and drained
1/3 cup sundried tomatoes packed in oil,
    oil drained (about 9)
1/2 cup pine nuts
1/4 cup grated parmesan cheese
3/4 cup olive oil (you can use some of the oil
    from the sundried tomatoes for extra flavor)
salt to taste

Boil pasta until just cooked, drain water and rinse with cold water to stop the cooking process. Set aside.

Combine pesto ingredients in a food processor. Puree to a grainy texture. Salt to taste.

Combine pasta with all of pesto, coating pasta well. Store in refrigerator until ready to serve.

Serves 8 - 12

Note: *This pesto is excellent on hot pasta as well.*

Broccoli with Breadcrumbs

- 1 lb broccoli, chopped
- 3 - 4 tbsp. olive oil
- 1/2 onion, minced
- 1 clove garlic, minced
- 3/4 cup breadcrumbs

In a small skillet, heat olive oil. Add onion, and saute until translucent. Add in garlic and breadcrumbs. Toast breadcrumbs until all of the oil has been absorbed. Set aside.

Bring water to a boil in a covered saucepan. Add in broccoli, cover and steam for 3-5 minutes. Drain water. Place in a serving dish.

Right before serving, pour breadcrumbs over broccoli.

Serves 4

Note: *If you double the amount of broccoli, I would not double the amount of breadcrumb topping.*

Flan de Cafe

(Coffee Caramel Custard)

Caramel:
1/4 cup water
1/2 cup sugar
5 drops lemon juice

Flan:
1 1/2 cups milk
1 14oz can condensed milk
3 eggs
3 egg yolks
1 tbsp. instant coffee granules

In a saucepan, combine the water, sugar and lemon juice. Bring to a boil, and simmer until the syrup turns dark. Pour into a 10" glass pie plate, spreading to cover as much of the bottom of the plate as possible. Set aside.

Fill a pitcher with water. Set aside. Find a baking pan in which your pie plate will fit. Set aside. Heat your oven to 325°.

Combine all of the flan ingredients in the container of a blender. Blend until smooth.

Place the baking pan in the oven. Using pitcher, fill the pan with 1" of water. Place prepared pie plate in the baking pan with the water. Fill the pie plate with the flan mixture. Close the oven, and bake the flan for 50 minutes, until a knife comes clean out of the center. Cool. Invert onto a platter before serving. (Can also be made in individual custard cups. Reduce cooking time to 35 minutes.)

Serves 8

Lime Butter Chicken

Lime Butter Chicken

Macaroni and Cheese with Tomatoes

Spinach with Peppered Vinegar

Cherry Pie

We always ate well when we went to Grandmother's house. I'd sit on two telephone books so I could reach my plate. The food was always typically Southern. Cornbread, black eyed peas, ham, biscuits and gravy... simple, yet good food. Grandaddy usually drank a glass of ice cold buttermilk with his meals, sometimes with salt and pepper on top. I can still see these foods on her table, as I peeked while we said grace.

Lime Butter Chicken

- 1 chicken, cut into halves
- 1 stick butter
- 2 limes
- salt to taste

Preheat broiler, with oven door ajar. Place chicken on broiler tray. Melt butter in a small saucepan, and squeeze in lime juice, adding the lime rinds to the butter. With a basting brush, baste chicken with the lime butter. Place in the oven under the hot broiler, on the lowest rack level. It should take 45 minutes for the chicken to cook. Turn over and baste as needed, so it will cook evenly, and not burn.

Serves 2 - 4

Note: *If you are using a lower oven, make sure there are no children or pets around. A broiler tray is a two piece tray. The top has long slits in it, the bottom is for catching the meat juices. You may want to line the broiler tray with foil, to facilitate clean-up. Don't forget to punch drain holes!*

Macaroni and Cheese with Tomatoes

1 lb elbow macaroni, or your favorite shape of dried pasta
4 tbsp. butter
2 tbsp. flour
3 cups milk
4 cups cheese, grated
    (about 1 lb – I use Cheddar or Monterrey Jack)
salt to taste
1 small onion, chopped
2 red tomatoes, cubed

Boil macaroni according to package directions. Drain and rinse with cold water to stop cooking process.

In a sauce pan, melt butter. Add in flour, and stir until smooth. Add in milk, and half of grated cheese. Stir and cook until thickened, about 10 minutes. When all the cheese is melted and the mixture is bubbling, add in the remaining cheese, salt, and the onion. Stir until cheese is melted. Remove from heat. Salt to taste.

Put cooled macaroni in a large casserole dish. Pour cheese sauce over macaroni, and top with chopped tomatoes. Cover, and bake for 30 minutes at 350°. Uncover, and bake for 10 more minutes.

Serves 8

Spinach with Peppered Vinegar

1 lb fresh spinach
pepper flavored vinegar

In a small amount of boiling water, steam about one pound of fresh spinach. Serve with a pepper flavored vinegar.

You can make your own peppered vinegar by combining you favorite hot chilies in a glass bottle with either white or apple cider vinegar. My grandmother used to use the piquin chilies that grew wild in her yard. She would pack a small cruet with the chilies, then fill it with white vinegar. The cruet was nice enough to set on the table. When all the vinegar had been poured off, she would simply refill it, until the pepper flavor began to weaken. Then she'd start all over again. It should take a couple of days for the vinegar to become saturated with flavor.

Serves 8

Cherry Pie

Pastry for a double crust 9" pie (see Basics)

Filling:
2 16oz cans tart cherries, reserve 1 cup
**   of cherry liquid**
1/3 cup cornstarch
1 1/2 cups sugar
1 tbsp. lemon juice
1/2 tsp. almond extract

Roll out half of pastry and line a 9" pie plate.
Roll out other half and set aside. Heat oven
to 375˚.

In a saucepan, stir together cherry liquid and
cornstarch. When cornstarch is dissolved, add
3/4 cup sugar. Heat mixture until thickened,
clear and bubbling. Add in remaining sugar,
lemon juice, almond extract, and drained
cherries. Stir to combine well.

Fill lined pie plate with cherry filling. Cover with
other half of rolled out pastry. Flute edges, trim
extra dough. Decorate top with remaining
dough. Make sure you puncture a few pressure
release holes into the top crust. Bake for 45
minutes until pastry is golden brown. Cool
before serving.

Serves 8

Sopa de Fideo

Sopa de Fideo
(Stewed Vermicelli Noodles)

Tostadas de Pollo
(Toasted Tortillas with Chicken)

Paletas de Tamarindo
(Tamarind Flavored Ice Pops)

Pink Limeade

You will notice that cooking *fideo* is just like making *carne guisada* (see *Guisado de Pollo*). They are both *guisados*, which, loosely translated, means "stews". In any *guisado*, first browning of the main ingredient occurs, then the sizzling addition of the stewing liquid.

Some folks like their *guisados* dry, some like them soupy. Neither one is more or less authentic. Add or subtract liquids as you like. Just make sure there is enough liquid to aid in cooking the main ingredient, without it scorching.

Tostadas con Pollo is quite the disorganized recipe, but I think that is what makes it my family's all time favorite lunches. The kids get to be creative, and the combinations seem endless. Use the refried beans as the first base layer of your tostada, so that your other additional ingredients "stick." Make sure the tostadas cool before you spread the beans on them. Otherwise, they get soggy, and it's crunch we're going for here.

This whole menu is dedicated to my kids, evident in the dessert of Tamarind Flavored Ice Pops.

Sopa de Fideo

(Stewed Vermicelli Noodles)

1 pkg fideo (vermicelli noodles)
3 tbsp. corn oil
1 medium onion, chopped
2 cups chicken broth
1 14oz can tomato puree
    or 2 fresh tomatoes, pureed in a blender
1 clove garlic, minced
1 serrano chile, optional
pinch ground comino
1 potato, cubed (optional)
cooked leftover meat, cubed (optional)

Brown fideo in oil along with onion. When the fideo is golden brown (not burnt), add remaining ingredients. Let simmer about thirty minutes. (If adding potato, make sure it is easily pierced with a fork.) Add more chicken broth if fideo reduces to the point of scorching.
Serve hot.

Serves 4 - 6

Tostadas de Pollo

(Toasted Tortillas with Chicken)

1 - 3 tortillas per person

Toppings:
refried pinto beans
leftover cooked chicken (beef or pork can be substituted)
grated cheese
sour cream
avocados
salsa picante or pico de gallo (see recipe pg. 74)
lettuce, tomato, and onion, chopped

Fry or bake the tortillas, according to your liking, to make them crisp (see Basics). Allow them to cool. Serve with the list of toppings, and allow everyone to concoct their own tostada.

Paletas de Tamarindo

(Tamarind Flavored Ice Pops)

1 lb tamarind pods (see Basics)
1 - 1 1/2 cups sugar (to taste)
5 cups water
ice cream sticks (found at craft stores)
3oz paper cups (bathroom size)

Peel tamarind pods, and place in a saucepan, covering the fruit with water. Bring water to a boil, and cook tamarind until soft, about 20 minutes. Drain water from fruit, reserving water. Press fruit through a mesh strainer, separating the pulp from the seeds. Discard seeds. You should end up with approximately 2 1/2 cups of pulp, including the reserved water.

Pour pulp and water into a blender. Add 5 cups of water to container, and sugar to taste. Blend well.

In a 9"x13" baking pan, place 24 3oz cups. Fill cups with prepared tamarind. Cover all the cups with one sheet of aluminum foil, smoothing over the top with your hand to show the edges of the cups. With an ice pick, poke a small hole in the foil over the exact center of the cup. This hole will make it easier to insert the ice cream stick through the foil. Insert ice cream sticks, then put baking pan in the freezer, making sure the sticks stay upright. Freeze overnight.

You may have a small amount of prepared tamarind left over. You can make a few extra paletas, or dilute it to make a couple of glasses of Agua de Tamarindo.

Makes approximately 24 paletas

Pink Limeade

3/4 cup lime juice (about 15 Mexican limes)
1/2 gallon water
1 cup sugar, or to taste
10 maraschino cherries
1/4 maraschino cherry syrup
rinds of juiced limes (about 4)

Combine all ingredients. Chill and serve over ice.

Makes about 1/2 gallon

Crab and Avocado Cakes

Crab and Avocado Cakes

Pear and Flower Salad

Minted Tea

Ursula's Cheesecake
with Apple Topping

Ursula is the mother of my college buddy, Eva. Ursula is from Germany, and created many a fine meal for her daughter's college friends (including me). On the weekends, we would point our vehicles in the direction of Long Island, in search of rest, relaxation, and a nice bagel. Not only did Eva's mom provide a haven for weary college women, but gave us counsel during our time away from our families.

Her cheesecake was always fabulous, so I asked her for her recipe. "Oh, a little of this, a little of that..." she would say. The original recipe ingredients are weighed, in the European style of cooking, which is more precise. However, I converted the recipe to cups for your convenience. The apple topping is my addition.

Crab and Avocado Cakes

- 1 lb crabmeat, picked over
- 1 avocado, peeled and chopped
- 1 shallot, minced
- 1 egg, beaten
- 2 tbsp. butter, softened
- 2 tbsp. lemon juice
- 1 tbsp. fresh dill, minced
- 3/4 cup bread crumbs
- salt and pepper
- pinch cayenne pepper
- olive oil, about 1/2 cup

Mix together crabmeat, avocado, shallot, egg, butter, lemon juice, dill, 1/4 cup bread crumbs, salt, pepper, and cayenne pepper. When well mixed, form into twelve cakes with hands.

Heat oil in a skillet. Gently dredge the crabcakes in the remaining bread crumbs, and fry in the heated oil. Turn over once. When golden brown, remove from pan and drain on paper towel.

Serves 4 - 6

Note: *Use two spatulas to turn over delicate crabcakes: Lift up a crabcake with one spatula, turn over onto the other spatula, then slide crabcake back into the hot oil.*

Pear and Flower Salad

Homemade mayonnaise:
1/2 tsp. dry mustard
1/4 tsp. paprika
pinch cayenne pepper
1 tsp. salt
2 egg yolks
2 tbsp. white vinegar
1 cup salad oil
2 tbsp. lemon juice

In a blender container, add mustard, paprika, cayenne pepper, salt, egg yolks, and vinegar. Start the blender, and begin to add oil, trickling it into the top feed hole of the blender as slowly as possible. Keep adding oil very slowly until you have a thick mayonnaise. Add in lemon juice.

Makes 2 1/2 cups

1 recipe homemade mayonnaise
4 very ripe pears, partially peeled, cored and halved
    (I like Bartletts)
3 - 4 handfuls *mesclun*
    (mixture of a variety of lettuces and greens)
2 oz crumbled blue cheese
edible flowers

Arrange pears on bed of greens, cored side up. Place dollop of mayonnaise in center hollow. Sprinkle cheese over, arranging flowers on top for color. Serve immediately.

Serves 6 - 8

Minted Tea

3 regular tea bags
2 mint tea bags
4 cups boiling water
4 cups room temperature water
ice, mint sprigs, lemon, sugar

Place all the tea bags in a heat proof pitcher. Pour boiling water over. Let steep for 3-5 minutes. Remove bags, then add remaining water. Serve over ice, with lemon and sugar, garnished with mint sprigs.

Makes 2 quarts

Ursula's Cheesecake with Apple Topping

Cake crust:
2 cups all purpose flour
1 stick butter, softened
1/2 cup sugar
1 egg
1 tsp. baking powder
1 envelope vanilla sugar or 1 tsp. vanilla extract

Cake Filling:
6 eggs, separated
1 cup sugar
3 8oz pkgs cream cheese
1 small, 4-serving pkg cook-and-serve vanilla pudding
    (not instant)
1 cup sour cream
1 tsp. vanilla

To make the crust: Combine all ingredients and mix to form firm pastry dough. Pat into a greased 9" springform pan, 1/2 inch thickness of dough on bottom and halfway up the side of the pan. Set aside.

To make the filling: Reserving egg whites, combine all remaining ingredients in a mixer until creamy and smooth. Beat egg whites until stiff, then fold into mixture. Pour into prepared crust in springform pan. Bake at 325° for 75 to 90 minutes, until cake has risen substantially. The crust will be a very dark brown, and cracked open in places. To test for doneness, use a toothpick, or shake cake slightly to see if center trembles. Cake is ready when middle appears firm.

Let cake cool slightly in pan, then loosen cake from edge of pan with a knife. Flip pan with cake still in it face down on a cake rack. Loosen the springform, and lift off removable bottom of pan. Retighten springform, and let cake cool, face down on rack. Later, flip cake over onto a plate and carefully remove springform, with a knife nearby to help with the parts that may have gotten stuck. Cooling the cake "bottom up" prevents a soggy crusted cake.

Serve with Apple Macadamia Sauce.

Serves 12

Apple Macadamia Sauce

4 - 6 tbsp. butter
6 - 8 Granny Smith Apples, peeled, sliced,
    and sprinkled with lemon juice
2/3 - 1 cup brown sugar
3 - 4 tbsp. macadamia nut liquor,
    or your favorite nut flavored liquor

Sauté apples in butter, then add brown sugar. Let sugar melt, then add liquor. Let bubble until you can no longer smell the alcohol. Serve warm over cooled cheesecake.

Bratwurst with Lentils

Bratwurst with Lentils
Pickled Beets
Potato Rolls
Chocolate Sheet Cake

German settlers came to this area with the promise of good and plentiful farmland. Many of them settled in the Hill Country, around San Antonio. Fredricksburg, Gruene and New Braunfels are the best known German settlements in Texas. This menu is definitely reminiscent of our German heritage.

Don't try using the microwave for boiling the ingredients in the cake recipe. I have. It doesn't work. This is a very easy cake, otherwise. It takes thirty minutes to make and bake this dessert. And best of all, you can tell everyone you made it from scratch.

Serve with: Iced Tea

B ratwurst with Lentils

- 1 lb lentils, picked over and rinsed
- 1 tomato, chopped
- 1 onion, chopped
- 1 clove garlic, peeled
- salt to taste
- 4 bratwurst sausage, about 1 lb
- 1 can beer

Place lentils in a pot, and cover with water (the amount of water needed is four times the amount of lentils to be cooked). Add in tomato, onion and garlic, and cook according to package directions, about 1 hour, or until tender. Salt to taste.

Meanwhile, heat your oven to 350°. Place bratwurst in a baking pan, and pour beer over sausage. Place in oven for 45 minutes, until sausage are browned on the outside.

Using a slotted spoon, transfer the cooked lentils to a serving dish. Arrange cooked bratwurst on top. Serve immediately.

Serves 4

otato Rolls

1/2 cup mashed potatoes
3/4 cup milk
1/2 cup water (preferably, water reserved from boiled
    potatoes)
4 tbsp. butter
1/4 cup sugar
1 tsp. salt
4 - 4 1/2 cups all purpose flour
2 pkgs yeast

In a small saucepan, combine mashed potatoes, milk, water, butter, sugar and salt. Stir and heat until smooth. Cool to 105˚ to 115˚.

In the bowl of a mixer, combine 2 cups of the flour with the yeast. Affix the dough hooks to the mixer. Pour in warm potato mixture, and begin mixing. Gradually add in enough of the remaining flour to make a soft dough. Knead for about 5 minutes. Gather up dough into a ball, and place in a greased bowl. Allow to rise for one hour.

Punch down dough, and let rest for 10 minutes. Shape dough into 24 balls, and place in a greased 9"x13" pan. With a flour sifter, dust the tops of the rolls with a little flour. Allow to rise for another 30-45 minutes.

Bake at 375˚ for 15-20 minutes.

Makes 24 rolls

ickled Beets

- 1 1/2 lbs beets
- 1 small onion, sliced
- 1 cup water
- 1 cup white vinegar
- 1 cup sugar
- 1 tsp. mustard seed
- 1 tsp. whole allspice
- 1 cinnamon stick
- 5 whole cloves

Trim greens from beets. Do not cut the beet root bulb. Leave the root tip intact, otherwise the beet will "bleed" while it is boiling. In a saucepan, boil beets until tender. Cool, then trim off top and tip, and peel. Cut into quarters, then place in a 1 quart glass or ceramic container. Add sliced onion to container.

In a small pan, combine the remaining ingredients. Bring to a full rolling boil, and cook for 5 minutes. Pour into container over beets and onions. Cap and refrigerate at least one week before eating. (This recipe can be processed in a water bath for shelf storage.)

Makes 1 quart

# Chocolate Sheet Cake

Cake:
4 tbsp. cocoa
1 stick butter or margarine
1/4 cup shortening
1 cup water
2 cups flour
2 cups sugar
1/2 cup buttermilk
1 tsp. baking soda
2 eggs, slightly beaten
1 tsp. vanilla

Frosting:
1 stick butter or margarine
4 tbsp. cocoa
6 tbsp. milk
1 lb powdered sugar
1 cup chopped pecans
1/2 tsp. vanilla

Heat oven to 400°. In a saucepan, bring cocoa, margarine, shortening, and water to a simmer. Pour mixture over flour and sugar in a large bowl. Mix well. Add buttermilk that has been mixed with soda. Mix well. Add beaten eggs and vanilla. Spray a 9"x13" pan with cooking spray. Add batter, and bake for 20 minutes or until toothpick comes out clean from center.

Five minutes before cake is finished, make frosting. Bring butter, cocoa, and milk to a simmer. Add powdered sugar, nuts and vanilla to cocoa mixture. Mix well, then pour over cake while cake and frosting are still hot.

Serves 16

Fried Eggs
With
Mild Green
Sauce

Fried Plantains

Atole de Fresa

page 50

Coconut
and
Vanilla Bean
Pudding

Tortilla Soup

page 54

Caldo de Mariscos

(Seafood Soup)

Tostadas Con Chile

page 65

Crab and Avocado Cakes

Pear and Flower Salad

Minted Tea

Ursula's Cheesecake with Apple Topping

page 88

Bratwurst with Lentils

Pickled Beets

Potato Rolls

Chocolate Sheet Cake

page 91

Shrimp Stuffed Avocados

Refresco Tropical
(Tropical Drink)

Blarney Stones

page 146

Strawberries
with
Rompope

page 152

Curried Shrimp and Artichoke Shortcake

Sweet Potato Biscuits

Black Eyed Pea Salad

Pecan Tassies

page 67

Cucumber With Creamy Mint Dressing

Spiced Tea

page 143

Flautas

(Flute Shaped Tacos)

Agua de Tamarindo
*(Refreshment
of Tamarind)*

Almond Scented
Macaroons

page 28

Chuletas Verdes Con Cebolla

(Green Pork Chops with Onions)

Monedas y Pepitas
(Carrot Coins with Pumpkin Seeds)

page 33

**Maple
Pecan
Overnight
Rolls**

page 151

Codorniz en Nogada

(Quail in Pecan Sauce)

Arroz con Rajas
(Rice with
Chile Strips)

**Spinach Salad with
Mustard Vinaigrette**

**Broiled Pineapple
with Piloncillo**

page 183

New Year's Eve

Puerco en Pipian
(Pork in Pumpkin Seed Sauce)

Black Eyed Peas

Arroz con Platanos
(Rice with Plantains)

Buñuelos
(Tortilla Fritters)

Margaritas en las Rocas
(Margaritas on the Rocks)

page 47

Rosca de Reyes

(Bread of the Kings)

page 132

Christmas Feast

Tamales Norteños

Menudo

Polvoron de Cacahuate
(Peanut Puffs)

Pepitoria
(Pumpkin Seed Brittle)

Galletas de Piloncillo
(Piloncillo Cookies)

page 114

Tools

1. Comal
2. Tortilla Press
3. Molcajete
4. Molinillo

Ingredients

1. Plantains
2. Cilantro
3. Queso Asadero
4. Epazote
5. Cactus *(nopalitos)*
6. Tamarind
7. Piloncillo
8. Tomatillos
9. Queso Fresco
10. Chayote Squash

Additional information on unfamiliar ingredients can be found in the recipe section.

Chilies

1. Dried Guajillo
2. Dried Ancho
3. Fresh Poblano
4. Dried Pasilla
5. Fresh Serrano
6. Fresh Jalapeño
7. Fresh Piquin
8. Dried Chipotle
9. Dried Arbol

How To Roll A Tamale

❶
Spread masa on corn husk, leaving 1 1/2" of husk clean to side. Place line of filling on masa.

❷
Fold edge of shuck over the filling.

❸
Roll tamale toward edge of shuck.

❹
Fold down top flap.

Christmas Feast

Tamales Norteños

Menudo

Polvoron de Cacahuate
(Peanut Puffs)

Pepitoria
(Pumpkin Seed Brittle)

Galletas de Piloncillo
(Piloncillo Cookies)

Everyone has their own Christmas traditions that are sacred unto that particular family. We have our own. Some traditions are simple, some religious, some are just downright weird, but our Christmas journey always follows a similar path.

Tamales are traditionally a Christmas food. They are quickly eaten, but time consuming to prepare. Get the whole family involved and have an old fashioned *tamalada* (*tamale* rolling party). After you prepare the meat and masa, call in friends and family members to help shape the tamales, just like a quilting bee.

Every region in Mexico has a *tamale* that is particular to that area. They differ in size and content tremendously. The recipe below is for our local version of the *tamale*.

Menudo is a staple for any midnight gathering, after Midnight Mass, after a wedding, etc... Noemi Vela taught me how to make menudo; my grandfather insists hers is the best. This is her recipe. She recommends using an electric turkey roaster to boil the tripe. Just remove the inner roasting pan and place the water and tripe directly in the roaster. Using a portable electric turkey roaster allows you to cook the tripe out on your porch. Tripe tends to be a bit (ahem) aromatic, and is better off cooking where there is plenty of circulating air. Cut the tripe in 2 to 2 1/2 inch squares. Any smaller, the tripe will dissolve while cooking; any larger would be beyond bite-sized.

Pepitoria is a candy made with pumpkin seeds. Don't add in any more than two cups of seeds, or flattening the candy will prove difficult. Try substituting raw sesame seeds for some of the pumpkin seeds for a different brittle.

The *Galletas de Piloncillo* are not too sweet, and can serve as the classic cut-out cookies everyone makes at Christmas. Use small animal shaped cookie cutters. The kids will love to make their own animal crackers.

Tamales Norteños

Meat:
4 - 5 lbs pork shoulder
1 onion
2 cloves garlic
2 bay leaves
salt to taste

Seasoning:
5 guajillo chilies
8 ancho chilies
1/2 cup pork broth
7 cloves garlic
1/2 lb pork lard
1/2 tsp. whole pepper
1/2 tsp. whole comino
salt to taste

Masa (dough):
1 4.4 lb pkg masa (instant corn tortilla mix)
1 tbsp. baking powder
2 tbsp. salt
2 1/2 lbs pork lard
7 1/2 cups pork broth

12 oz dried corn shucks (these must be soaked in water
    1 - 2 hours before use)

To prepare the filling: Boil the pork shoulder in a large stock pot with the onion, garlic, bay leaves and salt. When it is well cooked (about 1 hour of cooking time), remove the meat from the broth. Reserve broth for later use. Remove meat from the bones. Discard bones.

With a meat grinder, grind the cooked pork. (If you don't have a meat grinder, mince the meat as finely as possible with a knife, or grind in a food processor.)

To prepare the meat filling seasoning: Boil the chilies together until tender, about 15 minutes. Remove and discard the stems, and add chilies to the container of a blender. Add in the 1/2 cup pork broth and garlic, and puree well (add more broth if necessary to facilitate blending.) Strain puree through a wire strainer to extract any seeds.

In a spice grinder or *molcajete*, grind pepper, garlic, and comino with some salt. Make sure the mixture is finely ground. Set aside.

In a skillet, heat 1/2 lb lard. When melted, add the ground spice mixture, and saute for 20 seconds. Add in chili puree, and saute for 2 minutes. Add in ground pork, combining well. Adjust seasonings. Simmer for 10 minutes, then remove from heat. Set aside.

To prepare the Masa: Pour the contents of the package of masa into a very large bowl (I use a metal turkey roaster pan). Add in the baking powder and salt. Knead the lard in with your hands. Add in the broth one cup at a time. You may need a bit more or less broth. The masa is ready when the dough no longer sticks to your hands, and is smooth and delicate to the touch.

To assemble the tamales: Dry off some of the corn shucks, and place a few within reach. To make a proper tamale, the corn shuck bottom edge should be around 8 inches wide. Discard those that are too narrow, and tear bits off of the ones that are too wide. Take a corn shuck, and spread the bottom 2/3 of the leaf with 3 - 4 tablespoons of masa. Leave a 1 1/2" wide area along one edge free of masa. Spread the masa thinly. Place line of about 2 tablespoons of the filling, following the direction of the corn shuck veins, on the spread masa, towards the center of the prepared shuck. Fold the edge of the prepared shuck over the filling, then roll up towards the edge of the shuck with no masa. Fold down the top flap. Continue until all the tamales have been formed.

Place tamales in a large steamer basket. Boil water in the bottom of the steamer. As a top layer, cover the tamales with extra corn shucks, then with a sheet of plastic wrap. Secure the lid of the steamer, using foil around the edges of the lid to prevent the escape of steam. Place the steamer over the boiling water. Steam the tamales for about 40 minutes, until the masa is firm.

Makes 16 dozen

Note: *If you have leftover masa, you can make tamales out of refried beans instead of meat. Or concoct your own filling using leftover cooked chicken, beef, pork, or venison. Just mince or grind the meat, and add spices and a little leftover chile puree. Be creative. Write down what you do. You may like it and want to do it again!*

Menudo

20 lbs beef honeycomb tripe, rinsed and cut into
    2 to 2 1/2 inch squares
1 1/2 lbs fresh pigs feet
1 cup tequila
water
1/2 lb ancho chilies
1 head garlic, peeled
1 tbsp. whole comino
1 tbsp. whole black pepper
3 - 4 tbsp. salt
2 1/2 lbs fresh hominy (pozole) or three 1 lb 14oz cans
    of white hominy, drained
fresh or dried oregano
1 onion, chopped
limes cut in quarters

In a large pot or in an electric turkey roaster, place cut up pieces of tripe and pig's feet. Fill pot or roaster with water, barely covering the tripe. Add in tequila. Bring pot to a boil, and cook for about 1 1/2 hours.

Meanwhile, boil the ancho chilies until tender, about 15 minutes. Remove stems, and add to the container of a blender. Add just enough water to facilitate blending. Blend the chilies until you have a smooth paste. You will need 1 quart of ancho chile puree. Set aside.

Grind the garlic and spices in a *molcajete* or spice grinder until you have a fine paste. Add into menudo pot. Add in chile puree. Your

menudo should need about 30 minutes more of cooking time at this point. When the *pansitas* (tripe pieces) are fork tender, but slightly firm, remove the menudo from the heat. Add in the fresh or canned *pozole* (hominy).

Add in 1 - 2 tablespoons fresh or dried oregano, if desired, or serve oregano on the side. Serve with chopped onions and limes.

Serves 30

Pepitoria
(Pumpkin Seed Brittle)

1 1/2 cups raw, unsalted, shelled pumpkin seeds
butter
1 cup sugar
1 1/2 cups light corn syrup
1/2 cup water

Heat oven to 350°. Toast pumpkin seeds in the oven for about 8 minutes, until they start to pop. Set aside, but keep warm. Butter a large baking sheet well, preferably one with sides (16"x 10"x 1").

In a saucepan, add sugar, corn syrup, and water. Mix well, and begin to cook. Stir mixture as it begins to boil. Cook until it turns amber and reaches a temperature of 295°. Add in the pumpkin seeds quickly, stirring well. As quickly as possible, pour mixture onto prepared pan. Spread out thinly, using a greased spatula to press down mounds. Allow to cool completely. Break into pieces, and store in an airtight container.

117 *Makes about 2 lbs*

Polvoron de Cacahuate

(Peanut Puffs)

1 cup dry roasted peanuts
2 cups flour
1 cup sugar
2 tsp. baking soda
1 cup shortening

Heat oven to 350°. In a food processor, combine the peanuts and dry ingredients. Pulse until peanuts are finely ground. Add in shortening, and continue to process until you have a soft dough. Roll the dough into small balls, about 1 1/2" in diameter. Place on an ungreased cookie sheet. Bake for 10-12 minutes, until golden brown.

Makes about 4 dozen

Note: *If using a regular mixer, just mince the peanuts finely before adding to the remaining ingredients.*

Galletas de Piloncillo

(Piloncillo Cookies)

1 8oz *piloncillo* (see Basics)
1 stick cinnamon
5 whole cloves
1 cup water
1 orange, cut in half
4 cups flour
1 1/2 tsp. baking powder
1 cup butter or shortening

Glaze:
1 egg, beaten with one tsp. water

In a small saucepan, combine the *piloncillo*, cinnamon, cloves, water and orange halves. Bring to a boil. When the *piloncillo* has dissolved, remove from the heat and allow to cool. Squeeze the orange halves to extract the juice. Discard orange rinds. Strain out spices. You should have between 1 1/3 and 1 1/2 cups of liquid.

Combine the flour, baking powder and butter (or shortening) in a mixing bowl. Beat with an electric mixer. Add in the liquid a bit at a time until all is incorporated. Chill the dough for at least one hour.

Heat the oven to 350°. On a floured surface, roll out the cookie dough to 1/4 inch thickness. Cut into shapes with cookie cutters. Place on an ungreased cookie sheet. Brush with the egg mixture, or decorate as desired. Bake for 10-12 minutes. Cool completely before storing.

Makes 5 1/2 dozen 3" cookies

Whole Flounder Stuffed with Crab

Whole Flounder Stuffed with Crab

Mushrooms in
Garlic Hollandaise Sauce

Katy Kornettes

Chocolate Pound Cake

My dad loves to go down to South Padre Island. He relaxes, tries to catch fish, and beachcombs. My great grandmother beachcombed a lot. I can't figure out why they like to spend the day in the hot sun, wearing funky hats, and looking at their feet. I guess the beachcombing gene skips a generation.

Dad noticed that a lot of the seafood restaurants offered stuffed flounder, but it was usually a flounder filet wrapped around a bready filling. For my Dad, I had to make the genuine article.

The Katy Kornettes are famous in San Antonio. I have been trying to copy this recipe since I first had them back in high school. If you don't have a pastry bag, you can make do with a plastic food storage bag. Just fill the bag with the cooled batter, snip a small corner off of the bag with some scissors, and pipe away.

Be careful with the garlic sauce in the Mushroom recipe. It is very delicate, and will break if you attempt to cook it. Just heat it barely enough to melt the butter.

Whole Flounder Stuffed with Crab

2 - 3 lb whole flounder, scaled and cleaned

Stuffing:
3 tbsp. butter
1 shallot, minced
1 rib celery, minced
1 tbsp. flour
1/2 cup half and half
1/2 cup white wine
1/4 cup breadcrumbs
pinch cayenne pepper
8 oz fresh crabmeat, picked over (do not rinse)
salt and cracked black pepper

To prepare your fish for stuffing: With a sharp knife, make a horizontal cut down the body of the flounder, from gills to tail. Make a vertical cut just underneath the gills, extending to each edge of the fish. Your cuts should resemble a "T." Make the horizontal cut all the way down into the spinal column. With the tip of your knife, loosen one of the fillets from the rib bones, leaving the fillet attached at the edge of the fish. Do the same on the other side. You should now have a flounder that is opened down the center, with two flaps to fold over the stuffing.

Heat oven to 375°. Place fish in an oven proof dish. Season with salt and pepper.

In a saucepan, melt 3 tablespoons butter. Saute shallot and celery until translucent. Add in flour, and mix until well combined. Stir in cream, and allow mixture to thicken. Add in wine and cayenne pepper, and stir until sauce is thick and bubbling. Add in crab and breadcrumbs, stir well, then remove from heat. Salt and pepper to taste.

Fold back fillet flaps of prepared flounder. Accommodate as much of the stuffing possible inside the fish. Cover the stuffing with the flaps, then arrange the remaining stuffing over the opening. Cover the fish with foil, leaving the tail exposed (foil will stick to tail fin and ruin presentation). Bake for 25 minutes. Uncover, then bake for another 5 minutes, so that the fish will brown.

Serves 2

Mushrooms in Garlic Hollandaise Sauce

1 1/2 lbs fresh mushrooms, well washed

Sauce:
1 egg yolk
juice of one lemon or lime
1 4oz stick of butter, cut in half
1 - 2 cloves garlic, minced
1 - 2 tbsp. parsley, chopped

In a large pot, boil plenty of water. Add in mushrooms. Cover, and boil for 3 minutes. Drain water, and set aside.

In a heavy saucepan, whisk together egg yolk and lemon juice. Add 1/2 stick of butter, and heat over a very low flame. Whisk quickly to melt butter, but do not raise flame. When butter is just melted, remove from heat. Do not simmer or "cook" as sauce will break. Add in remaining butter and garlic, and stir until butter is melted. Add parsley.

Pour sauce over mushrooms and serve immediately.

Serves 4 - 6

Katy Kornettes

1 qt milk
3 cups cornmeal
1 cup butter
1 cup sugar
1 tsp. salt

In a large heavy saucepan, boil milk. As milk comes to a boil, sift cornmeal into milk with a flour sifter in one hand, and a spoon in the other, stirring briskly. Mixture should still be cooking while sifting in the cornmeal. When mixture becomes to difficult to stir, stop sifting in cornmeal, turn off heat, and add in butter, sugar and salt. Resume sifting and stirring until all the cornmeal has been added. If you notice any lumps in your mixture, whip with an electric hand mixer until smooth. Let stand 5 minutes.

Heat oven to 350°. Spoon mixture into a pastry bag; no tip is necessary. Pipe out small peaked mounds (like chocolate kisses), 1 1/2" in diameter, onto an ungreased cookie sheet. Bake for 25 minutes, or until golden brown.

Makes about 6 dozen

Note: *This recipe can be cut in half.*

Chocolate Pound Cake

- Cake:
- 3 cups flour
- 1/2 tsp. baking powder
- 1/2 cup cocoa
- 1/2 tsp. salt
- 1 cup butter
- 1/2 cup shortening
- 3 cups sugar
- 5 eggs
- 1 cup milk
- 1 tsp. vanilla

- Glaze:
- 1 cup powdered sugar
- 2 tbsp. cocoa
- 2 tbsp. cream or milk

Heat oven to 325°. Sift together flour, baking powder, cocoa and salt. Set aside. Cream together butter, shortening and sugar. Add in eggs. Alternately add in milk and flour mixture. Stir in vanilla.

Pour batter into a 10" floured and greased bundt pan. Bake for 1 hour, or until a toothpick comes clean out of center. Cool.

When cake is cool, stir together glaze ingredients until smooth. Drizzle over the top of the cake.

Serves 12

Lengua Entomatada

Lengua Entomatada
(Beef Tongue in Tomato Sauce)

Chayotes Rellenos de Elote
(Stuffed Chayote Squash)

Moros y Cristianos
(Moors and Christians)

Fresh Orange Chill

Lengua Entomatada makes a frequent appearance at my in-law's house. "*Entomatada*" directly translated means "that which has been tomatoed." If you have never had stewed beef tongue, you should try this recipe. The meat is tender, and the sauce is fabulous over rice. Making small taquitos of the meat on hot, fresh corn tortillas is a trip to heaven.

Moros y Cristianos is a traditional dish, composed of black beans and rice. This is a great dish for vegetarians, in that it is a complete protein, combining rice and beans. You can substitute white rice for the brown rice; just reduce the cooking time to 25 minutes.

Serve with: *corn tortillas*

L engua Entomatada

(Beef Tongue in Tomato Sauce)

1 beef tongue, about 3 lbs

Sauce:
1 1/2 lbs fresh tomatoes
water
2 tbsp. oil
1 onion, sliced
2 cloves garlic
3 tbsp. capers
3/4 cup green olives stuffed with pimentos
salt
1 bay leaf

Boil beef tongue in a large stock pot for about 2-3 hours, adding water as necessary. When beef tongue is cool, peel off tough outer layer, and remove root. Cut into 1/2 inch thick slices.

Puree tomatoes and garlic in a blender, with enough water to facilitate blending. Heat oil in a large pan, and saute onion until translucent. Add tomato puree, capers, olives, salt and bay leaf. Simmer sauce, reducing it by about 1/3. Add in tongue slices, and cover. Simmer another 15-20 minutes.

Serves 4

Note: *This is yet another dish that tastes better the second day. If you would like to make this dish a day in advance, you may wish to skip simmering the meat in the sauce. Just reduce the sauce for 20 minutes as directed, then pour sauce over sliced tongue. Allow to cool, then store in refrigerator.*

Moros y Cristianos

(Moors and Christians)

4 cups broth from cooked black beans,
     or water, or a combination of the two
1/2 onion, chopped
2 cloves garlic
2 tbsp. oil
2 cups brown rice, uncooked and rinsed
1 cup black beans, cooked
salt to taste
4 - 5 leaves of epazote

Place broth, onion, and garlic in a blender. Puree well and set aside.

Heat oil in a skillet. Add the brown rice to warm (not hot) oil. Fry raw rice for about 7 minutes, until rice begins to look opaque. Add in puree. Bring mixture to a boil. Add in beans, salt and epazote, and stir to combine. Cover tightly, and simmer for 35 minutes over a low flame.

Serves 8

Chayote Rellenos de Elote

(Chayote Squash Stuffed with Corn)

4 *chayote* squash
1 poblano chile
2 tbsp. chopped onion
1 tbsp. oil
1 carrot, grated
2 ears fresh corn, kernels cut off of cob
4 oz cream cheese
2/3 cup sour cream

Boil *chayotes* whole in a large pot for one hour. Remove from water and allow to cool.

Roast poblano chile in the flame of a gas stove, or under broiler in oven. The skin of the chile should be evenly blackened and blistered. Peel chile, remove and discard stem and seeds (see Basics). Chop chile into small squares.

Meanwhile, heat oil in a skillet. Sauté onion with grated carrots, about 2 minutes. Add remaining ingredients, including chopped poblano chile, and combine well until cheese is melted. Salt to taste. Remove from heat.

Cut cooled *chayotes* in half lengthwise. Remove center pit and pod surrounding it. Reserve the almond shaped pit. With a spoon, scoop out *chayote* flesh. Cut up the removed flesh, and add to the cheese mixture, combining well.

Heat oven to 350°. Fill *chayote* shells with cheese mixture. Heat *chayotes* in oven for about ten minutes. Remove from oven, then place *chayote* seed on top. Serve immediately.

Serves 8

resh Orange Chill

- **8 cups fresh orange juice**
- **6 envelopes unflavored gelatine**
- **1 star fruit (*carambola*)**

Pour gelatin into a bowl. Heat 4 cups of orange juice until boiling. Pour over gelatin. Stir until gelatin is dissolved, about 2 minutes. Add in remaining orange juice, stir, and transfer to a 10 cup ring mold. Chill in the refrigerator for at least 4 hours, until gelatin is firm.

To unmold gelatin, place mold in a sink filled with hot water (do not get gelatin wet). Remove after 5-10 seconds. Invert mold on platter. Garnish with slices of star fruit.

Serves 8

Easter Feast

Rosemary Pork Loin

Glazed Carrots with Pistachios

Refresco De Manzana
(Fresh Apple Drink)

Deviled Eggs with Corn Relish

Coconut Angel Food Cake

Every time my family comes down to the ranch to visit, Mom makes a roast. She puts it on in the morning, slowly filling the house with a beautiful aroma. By noontime, we look like a bunch of cartoon characters, pathetically crawling towards the kitchen, hoarsely whispering "Lunch... lunch..." As usual, she steps over our bony bodies, and continues her busy schedule in the kitchen.

Actually, we all pitch in with the work detail. I am usually cooking with Mom. Mary Margaret and Elizabeth are either decorating the table or making dessert. James is loafing around with the brethren-in-law, and Stephanie would be defending the deviled eggs from Dad.

Easter is a time of rebirth and rejoicing. It is also an important time to gather with the people that gave you and witnessed your life. I love to watch my little guys hunt for Easter eggs. That is the greatest joy I know.

 # Rosemary Pork Loin

- 1 pork loin roast, about 4 lbs with bones
- 1 sprig rosemary
- salt and pepper
- your favorite seasoning mix (I use Cavender's Greek Seasoning)
- 2 cups red wine

Heat the oven to 325°. Place roast in a metal roasting pan, bone side down. Cut slits 1/2 inch deep and 1 inch apart across the top fat layer of the roast. Remove the rosemary leaves from their stem, and stuff the leaves into the slits on the roast. Season the top of the roast with salt, pepper, and a seasoned salt mix. Place roast in oven.

The roast should take 30 minutes per pound to cook, or to reach an internal temperature of 170°. During the last hour of cooking, pour red wine over roast. Return roast to oven, basting roast every 15 minutes. Roast will carve more easily if allowed to cool slightly before serving.

Even though this menu doesn't call for gravy, you can make gravy from the drippings. Skim off all but about 3 tablespoons of oil. Scrape up browned bit from the sides and bottom of pan. Heat roasting pan on the stove. Mix together 3 cups water and 2/3 cup flour. When drippings are simmering, pour in flour mixture. Stir until gravy is uniformly colored and thick. Season to taste.

Note: *Do not use a glass or ceramic baking dish if you plan to make gravy in the same pan on the stove top. The dish will break.*

Serves 6

Deviled Eggs with Corn Relish

1 dozen eggs, hard boiled
1/3 cup purchased corn relish, or see recipe below
1/4 cup mayonnaise
2 tbsp. dijon mustard
salt and pepper
fresh parsley or dill

Cut eggs in half lengthwise. Scoop out yolk. Arrange whites on a platter. Mash yolks until smooth, then add remaining ingredients. Refill egg white halves with mixture. Garnish with fresh parsley or dill.

Makes 24 eggs

Quick Corn Relish

- 1/2 onion, chopped
- 2 tbsp. olive oil
- 2 ears fresh corn, kernels removed
- 1/4 cup chopped red pepper
- 1/4 tsp. celery seed
- pinch ground tumeric

Saute the onion in the olive oil in a skillet. Add corn, red pepper and seasoning. Saute for about 7 minutes, until corn is tender.

Makes 1 pint

Refresco de Manzana

(Fresh Apple Drink)

2 - 3 Red Delicious apples, cored (not peeled)
    and cut into quarters
4 cups water
1/4 cup lemon juice
1/2 cup sugar
2 cups water

Combine apples and 4 cups water in a blender.
Puree well. Filter puree through a wire sieve
into a pitcher, pressing pulp to extract all the
liquid. Discard pulp. Add lemon juice, sugar and
remaining water. Mix well. Add more sugar,
water, or lemon juice, to taste.

Makes about 2 quarts

Glazed Carrots with Pistachios

1 1/2 lbs carrots, peeled and cut into thin circles
2 tbsp. butter
2 tbsp. honey
2 tsp. lime juice
1/2 cup shelled pistachios, crushed

Fill a covered skillet half full of water, and bring
to a boil. When water is boiling, add carrots.
Cover and cook until tender, but still slightly
firm. Pour carrots and water though colander.

In same skillet, melt butter. Add honey, and
mix well over low heat. Add in lime juice. When
glaze is well combined, return cooked carrots
to the skillet, and add pistachios. Toss well
until carrots are evenly coated with the glaze
and nuts.

Serves 8

Coconut Angel Food Cake

Cake:
1 1/8 cups cake flour
3/4 cup sugar
1 1/2 cups eggs whites (about 12 egg whites),
    room temperature
1/2 tsp. salt
1 1/2 tsp. cream of tartar
1 cup sugar
1 tsp. vanilla extract
1 tsp. almond extract

Heat oven to 375˚. Sift together cake flour and 3/4 cup sugar. Set aside. In a mixer bowl, add egg whites and salt, and begin to beat at top speed. When foamy, add in cream of tartar. Beat until stiff peaks begin to form, then gradually add in 1 cup sugar as mixer is still beating. Add in vanilla and almond extracts. When egg whites are beaten to their fullest (not dry), turn off mixer and remove bowl. Quickly fold in flour mixture.

Pour into an ungreased 10" tube pan. Bake for 30-35 minutes. Cool inverted on a cake rack.

Frosting:
3 egg whites
2 1/4 cups sugar
1/3 cup cold water
1/8 tsp. salt
2 1/4 tsp. light corn syrup or 1/4 tsp. cream of tartar
1 tsp. vanilla
1 cup sweetened shredded coconut

Place egg whites, sugar, water, salt and corn syrup or cream of tartar in the top of a double boiler. Place over boiling water. Begin to beat slowly with an electric hand mixer. When mixture becomes foamy and opaque, beat at the highest speed until stiff peaks form. Remove from heat and add vanilla. Cool slightly.

Spread frosting over cooled cake. Sprinkle coconut over surface of frosting. For extra texture, toast the coconut in the oven until lightly browned before sprinkling on the cake.

Serves 10 - 12

To use up egg yolks, see the recipe for *rompope (page 131)*.

Epiphany Feast

Pavo en Mole Poblano
(Turkey in Mole Poblano)

Rompope
(Mexican Style Eggnog)

Chicharones en Salsa Verde
(Pork Rinds in Green Sauce)

Rosca de Reyes
(Bread of the Kings)

January 6, The Feast of the Epiphany, is the day the Three Wise Kings arrived to adore the Baby Jesus. Historically, this day is more celebrated in Mexico than Christmas Day. A special sweet bread is made for the Feast of the Epiphany, which is called *Rosca de Reyes*. A small figurine of the Baby Jesus in hidden in the bread. The person who gets the slice of bread with the Baby Jesus doll is then required to throw a party on February 2, which is the Feast of the *Virgen de la Candelaria*.

What gives *mole* the reputation of being difficult to prepare is the assembly of the ingredients. The actual preparation is tedious, but not complicated. There are many types of *mole*, but this is the classic *mole*, Puebla style, that you would be served in a restaurant.

Mexican eggnog is very different from the traditional English style eggnog served during the holidays in the States. Try *rompope* for a change.

"Tu piensas que solo tus chicharones truenan" is my favorite saying in Spanish. It means "You think only your pork rinds crackle." This line is directed towards egomaniacs. Anyway, the sauce you pour over the pork rinds for the *Chicharones en Salsa Verde* will make them pop and crackle.

And you? How loud are your pork rinds?

Serve with: Rice, tortillas

Pavo en Mole Poblano
(Turkey in Mole Poblano)

1 10-15 lb fresh uncooked turkey
onions
garlic
salt

Sauce:
3 chipotle chilies
1/2 lb ancho chilies, stems removed
1/2 lb pasilla chilies, stems removed
1 lb tomatoes

Oil for frying
2 onions, chopped
8 cloves garlic, chopped
1 large plantain, peeled and sliced into rounds
1/4 lb raw peanuts
1/4 lb blanched almonds
1/4 lb sesame seeds
5 whole cloves

4 peppercorns
1 tsp. anise seed
1 tsp. coriander seed
1 tbsp. salt
2 tbsp. oil
3 toasted tortillas (see Basics for baked tostadas)
2 tbsp. sugar
1/4 cup raisins
1/2 cup pitted dried prunes
1 cup corn oil
3 - 4 qts turkey broth
8 oz Mexican chocolate
1 stick cinnamon
1/2 cup sesame seeds for garnish

Cut turkey to fit into a stock pot (you may need a couple of pots). Place a peeled, quartered onion in each pot, and one peeled clove of garlic. Boil turkey until it is cooked, about 1 hour. Salt to taste. Save the broth. Remove turkey from broth, cool, then remove turkey meat from bones, cutting them in large chunks. Cover, and store in refrigerator until ready for use.

Place all chilies and tomatoes in a saucepan and cover with water. Bring to a boil, and cook for 10 minutes. Drain water, and peel tomatoes. Place chilies and tomatoes in a very large bowl. Set aside.

Add 2 to 3 tablespoons of oil to a large skillet. Fry onions and garlic until translucent. Remove garlic and onions from the oil, and add to the large bowl with chilies.

In the same oil and skillet, fry the slices of plantain until golden on both sides. Remove slices to the large bowl.

- Add in 2-3 tablespoons of oil to the skillet. Add in peanuts, almonds, and sesame seeds. Fry nuts until slightly browned. Pour entire content of skillet into the large bowl.

- In a *molcajete* or spice grinder, grind cloves, peppercorns, anise and coriander seeds and salt into a fine powder. In a small, clean skillet, heat about 2 tablespoons of oil. Add in ground spices, and fry for 30 seconds. Pour spices and oil into the large bowl.

- Crumble the toasted tortillas and add to the large bowl, along with the raisins, prunes, and sugar. In a large stock pot, add one cup of oil, and heat.

- The sauce now needs to be blended until smooth: Fill a blender container 3/4 full with the mixture in the large bowl. Add in two cups of turkey broth, and blend until you have a smooth sauce, with no visible particles. Pour sauce into the stock pot with the heated oil. Continue processing the contents of the bowl with the turkey broth in this fashion until the entire contents of the bowl have been utilized. Add the chocolate and cinnamon stick to the stock pot. Simmer the sauce for 30 minutes.

- When ready to serve, place cooked turkey in a large dutch oven, or in a large open terra cotta *mole* dish. Cover the turkey with the *mole*. Stir a few times to turn the meat in the sauce. Heat well. Just before serving, sprinkle sesame seeds over the top.

- *Serves 12*

Rompope

(Mexican-Style Eggnog)

1/2 cup blanched almonds
6 cups whole milk
2 1/2 cups sugar
2 sticks cinnamon
2 cups rum
12 egg yolks

In a blender, combine the almonds and a cup of the milk. Puree until very smooth.

In a large saucepan, combine the almond milk, remaining milk, sugar and cinnamon. Heat over medium flame, until thickened and bubbling, stirring constantly.

Whip together egg yolks and rum with and electric hand mixer. While whipping, add in about a cup of the hot mixture, one spoonful at a time. Return egg mixture to the saucepan, and cook for another 2-3 minutes. Cool *rompope*, then store in refrigerator. Serve in small liquor glasses.

Makes about 2 quarts

Chicharones en Salsa Verde

(Pork Rinds in Green Sauce)

Sauce:
28oz can tomatillos (do not drain water)
2 cloves garlic
1 pickled jalapeño
2 tbsp. oil
1/2 onion, sliced
4 oz bag pork rinds

Combine tomatillos with their liquid, garlic, and jalapeño in a blender. Puree until smooth. Heat oil in a skillet, and add onions. When the onions are translucent, add in pureed tomatillos. Simmer for about 20 minutes, until the sauce is slightly reduced.

Place pork rinds in a serving dish. Pour sauce over right before serving. Do not add salt to the sauce as the pork rinds are usually salty.

Serves 8

Rosca de Reyes
(Bread of the Kings)

6 - 7 cups flour
3/4 cup sugar
2 pkgs yeast
1 tsp. salt
1/2 cup milk
1/2 cup water
1/2 cup butter
3 eggs
3 egg yolks
2 tbsp. orange flower water

Topping:
6 tbsp. margarine, softened
1/2 cup powdered sugar
2 egg yolks
3/4 cup flour

crystallized fruit in Christmas colors
   (cherries, pineapple, figs, etc)
1 small baby doll, 1 - 2 inches long

Combine the 2 cups of the flour, the sugar, yeast and salt in the bowl of a mixer. Affix the mixer with dough kneading hooks. Heat the milk, water and butter until the butter is melted and the liquid reaches a temperature between 105° and 115°. Add liquid to the flour mixture. Start the mixer, and add in the eggs, egg yolks, and orange flower water. Add in enough of the remaining flour until a stiff dough forms. Allow the dough to knead for 8-10 minutes. Remove bowl from mixer. Transfer dough to a greased bowl, and allow to rise for 1 hour, until it has doubled in bulk.

After the dough has risen, punch dough down. Allow dough to rest 5-10 minutes.

Shape bread dough into a ring in the following manner: Make a large round "patty" with the bread dough. Press a hole in the center. You should now have a fat doughnut shaped piece. Stretch doughnut to make an oval shaped ring, with a large hole in the center. The ring sides should be about 4 1/2"- 5" wide (the *rosca* somewhat resembles the shape of a horse-racing track!) Place shaped *rosca* on a greased pan, and allow to rise for another hour, until doubled in bulk.

Meanwhile, combine topping ingredients, and mix into a soft dough. Set aside.

When the shaped *rosca* is fully risen, heat oven to 350°. Decorate the top of the *rosca* with the topping dough, making circle and stripe shaped pieces, and pressing them lightly onto the *rosca*. Decorate with the colored crystallized fruit. Bake for 30 minutes, or until brown. Remove from oven, and let cool slightly.

With a knife, make a slit underneath the *rosca*. Press the baby doll up into the *rosca*.

Serves 24

Oyster and Roasted Garlic Soup

Oyster and Roasted Garlic Soup
Buttery Toast
Artichoke and Palm Heart Salad
Lemon Nut Pound Cake

Oyster and Roasted Garlic Soup has a very mellow flavor, in spite of its name. The added chilies give the soup a nice flavor, a great presentation, but no fire. Eating the chile would change the situation entirely.

Oyster and Roasted Garlic Soup

2 heads garlic
1 onion
8 green onions, chopped
2 tbsp. butter
1/4 cup flour
1 quart oysters, shucked, drained, liquor reserved

- 2 cups half and half
- 2 cups whole milk
- 2 cups chicken broth
- 2 cups oyster liquor (add more chicken broth if you don't have enough)
- 4 fresh whole green or red chilies (optional – I use serrano chilies)
- dry sherry

Heat oven to 350°. Place unpeeled whole garlic heads and unpeeled whole onion in a baking pan, and place in the oven for one hour.

When garlic and onion are roasted, remove from oven. Carefully cut the top off of each garlic head. Squeeze whole garlic head to release the roasted garlic pulp. Discard papery peel. Cut the top off of the onion, and peel. Cut in half. Place garlic, onion, and half and half in a blender. Puree well and set aside.

Chop oysters into bite sized pieces, and set aside.

Saute green onions in butter in a 4 quart stock pot. Add flour and stir until flour absorbs all of butter. Add in garlic puree, milk, chicken broth, and oyster liquor. Add in whole chilies, if desired. Simmer soup for about 10 -15 minutes, stirring so that it doesn't scald. Add in oysters, simmering about another 10 minutes. Serve hot, offering the dry sherry as an optional flavoring that you guests can add to their liking. Serve one chile in each bowl.

Serves 4

Buttery Toast

Butter slices of your favorite bread and place under broiler until well browned. Rub with minced garlic, top with herbs, or add a little grated parmesan cheese before broiling for variety. Using the oil from a jar of sundried tomatoes instead of butter is out of this world.

Artichoke and Palm Heart Salad

1 6.5oz jar marinated artichoke hearts, liquid reserved
1 14oz can hearts of palm, drained
1/2 cup olives stuffed with pimento
1 head Boston bibb lettuce

Reserve marinating liquid from the jar of artichokes. Chop artichokes, hearts of palm, and olives. Mix together. Arrange lettuce leaves on a platter. Mound chopped vegetables in the center of the platter. Just before serving, pour artichoke liquid over the top of the vegetables.

Serves 8

Lemon Nut Pound Cake

- 2 cups flour
- 1 tsp. baking powder
- 1/2 tsp. salt
- 1 1/4 cups sugar
- 3/4 cup butter
- 1/2 cup milk
- 3 eggs
- 1 tbsp. lemon rind
- 2 tbsp. lemon juice
- 1/2 cup chopped pecans

Heat oven to 350°. Sift together flour, baking powder and salt. Set aside. Cream together sugar, butter, milk and eggs. When smooth, add in flour mixture, lemon rind and lemon juice. Fold in pecans.

Grease the inside bottom of 9"x 5"x 2" loaf pan, not greasing the sides. Pour in the batter. Bake for 50-60 minutes, until a toothpick comes out clean from the middle. Remove from pan after 10 minutes, then cool completely before slicing.

Serves 12

Mole de Olla

Mole de Olla
(Pot Mole)

Kale with Lime Juice

Apple Crumb Pie

My husband's family loves chile, so I thought they would like this *Mole de Olla*. This has the possibilities of being an extremely spicy dish. I have adjusted down the amount of chilies used in this recipe to a moderate level. If you like things very hot, go ahead and add in more chilies.

This is a "Pot Mole" in that it doesn't require the elaborate preparation that *Mole Poblano* needs. It is a simple stew, with chilies. Feel free to add in other vegetables, such as corn on the cob, or Swiss chard.

If you have never tried kale, you will be pleasantly surprised. It has a rich flavor, like broccoli.

Serve with: tortillas or tostadas, beans and rice

Mole de Olla
(Pot Mole)

- 3 lbs pork shoulder, with bone
- 1 onion, coarsely chopped
- 2 garlic cloves, minced
- 1 bay leaf
- salt and pepper
- 2 whole cloves
- 3 carrots, peeled and chopped
- 2 chayote squash, chopped
- 10 dried chipotle chilies
- 2 ancho chilies
- 2 pasilla chilies
- 3 tomatoes
- 1 sprig epazote

In a 4 1/2 quart pot, add pork, onion, garlic, bay leaf, salt, pepper, and cloves. Fill pot with water, and bring to boiling point. Simmer until pork is cooked, about 40 minutes. Remove pork from broth and allow to cool for easy handling. Cut meat from bone, and cut meat into bite sized pieces. Return meat and bones to pot. Add in carrots and chayote, and simmer until tender, about 20 minutes.

Meanwhile, in a small saucepan, boil tomatoes and chilies, about 15 minutes. When they are tender, remove from water and place in a blender container. (Remove seeds from chilies if you would like a less spicy dish). Add about 2 cups of the pork broth. Puree well, then return puree to the pot. Add in epazote, and adjust salt, if necessary.

Serves 4

K **ale with Lime Juice**

2 bunches fresh kale, well washed
2 - 3 tbsp. oil
1 small onion, chopped
1 clove garlic
juice of one lime

In a saucepan, boil kale for about 20 minutes. Drain water.

Heat oil in a pan. add in the onion, and sauté until translucent. Add in garlic, lime juice, and cooked kale. Saute for about 10 minutes.

Serves 4

Apple Crumb Pie

Pastry for a single 9" pie crust (see Basics)

Filling:
2 1/2 lbs Granny Smith apples (about 7)
juice of one lemon
2/3 cup sugar
1/2 cup flour
1 tsp. ground cinnamon
pinch ground mace
pinch ground cardamom

Crumb Top:
3/4 cup butter, soft
2/3 cup sugar
1 1/2 cups flour
pinch ground cinnamon

Roll out pastry and line a 9" pie plate, fluting edges. Set aside.

Peel and slice apples into a bowl containing lemon juice. Mix in the remaining filling ingredients. When well mixed, fill lined pie plate.

Combine ingredients for crumb topping until the mixture resembles small peas. Top the pie with the mixture, accommodating the crumbs all the way to the edge of the pie.

Bake at 350° for 45-50 minutes. Cool before serving.

Serves 8

Pescado con Ajonjolí

Pescado con Ajonjolí
(Fish in Packets with Sesame Seed Crust)

Mixed Greens with Raspberry Vinaigrette and Parmesan Curls

Crepas de Cajeta
(Crêpes with Caramel Sauce)

Grilling fish on a fire is easy. If you are on a camping trip, you can cook your fish as directed in the recipe below, adding in whatever seasonings you might have on hand. Sometimes I'll put in a few lemon slices, a whole green chile, and a sliced scallion. The flavor combinations are endless. The sesame seed crust used here is simple, and gives your fish a nice texture.

Cajeta is a candy made with goat's milk that is very popular in Mexico. It is sold in jars or in small wooden boxes. A spoon is needed to eat *cajeta;* it is a rich, velvety caramel. Look for *cajeta* in a gourmet store in the candy or dessert sauce section. Making *cajeta* in the home takes over two hours of stirring. I recommend trying the store bought version before you attempt to make *cajeta* at home. Substitute a store bought caramel sauce if you can't find *cajeta.*

Pescado con Ajonjolí

(Fish in Packets with Sesame Seed Crust)

4 fish filets, or small whole fish (I use whole
   rainbow trout with the heads and tails)
3/4 cup sesame seeds
1/3 cup parsley, chopped
salt
pepper
aluminum foil

Lightly toast sesame seeds in a saute pan, about 4 minutes (no oil necessary). Arrange each fish on a piece of aluminum foil. Divide sesame seeds and fresh parsley between the four fish, sprinkling over the top. Season to taste. Fold foil to make a packet, and place on heated barbecue grill for 10 - 15 minutes. Place a packet on each plate.

Serves 4

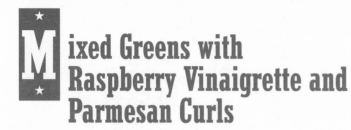

Mixed Greens with Raspberry Vinaigrette and Parmesan Curls

1 handful of mixed greens per person
ungrated Parmesan cheese (preferably Parmigiano Regianno)
1/2 cup olive oil
2 tsp. raspberry jam
salt
pepper
3 tbsp. raspberry vinegar

Arrange greens in salad bowl, or on individual plates. Scrape knife across block of parmesan cheese, so that cheese will shave off in small curls. Add about 2 teaspoons of cheese per person.

Whisk together the oil, jam, salt and pepper. When this is well combined, and the lumps of jam are dissolved, whisk in vinegar. Make sure mixture appears homogeneous. Pour dressing over salad right before serving.

Serves 4

Crepas de Cajeta

(Crêpes with Caramel Sauce)

Crêpes:
1 tbsp. butter, melted
2 cups milk
1 egg, beaten
1 1/2 cups flour

Sauce:
1 cup prepared *cajeta*
1/4 cup milk or orange juice
1/2 cup pecans, chopped
1 - 2 tbsp. brandy (optional)

Orange zest for garnish

To make the crêpes: Beat together the butter and milk. Whisk in egg. Sift flour into milk mixture at bit at a time, whisking to mix. Try to break up any lumps, however, a few lumps are okay.

Heat a shallow teflon pan, or a crêpe pan. Pour in about 1/3 cup of the batter, swirling the pan so that the bottom has a thin layer of the batter. Return to the heat for 60 seconds. Flip crepe, and cook on other side for 60 seconds. Remove crepe to a plate, and continue making crêpes in this fashion. One recipe of batter makes 8 - 9 crêpes.

For the *cajeta* (right before serving): In a saucepan, add in the *cajeta*, milk or juice, pecans and brandy. Stir and heat until thin. Fold one crêpe in half, then in half again to form a triangle. Place on a platter. Fold remaining crêpes, and overlap them on the platter. Pour *cajeta* sauce over. Garnish with orange zest.

Serves 8

Home Cured Pork

Home Cured Pork with Turnips

Cucumber with Creamy Mint Dressing

Spiced Tea

Apple Dumplings

This is another menu reminiscent of our German heritage. The home cured pork tastes a lot like corned beef. It is great cold or hot, or in sandwiches. Out of all the recipes in this book, this was my father-in-law's favorite.

You may have some extra mint dressing left over. Use it as a vegetable dip, or over boiled potatoes. It is a treat.

Serve with: steamed green beans or spinach, sliced homemade bread

Home Cured Pork with Turnips

- 5 lb pork shoulder roast
- 8 cups water
- 2 cups Morton's Tender Quick
- 1 tsp. whole mustard seeds
- 1 tsp. whole allspice
- 1 tsp. whole peppercorns
- 1 tsp. coriander seeds
- 5 juniper berries, crushed
- 3 bay leaves
- 2 cloves garlic
- 1 onion
- 10 whole cloves
- 2 lbs turnips, rutabagas or potatoes, peeled and quartered

To make the curing solution, dissolve the Tender Quick in 8 cups of water. Place pork in a non-reactive bowl large enough to accommodate the meat and the curing solution. The meat must be completely covered by the solution. Add in the mustard, allspice, peppercorns, coriander seeds, juniper berries, bay leaves and garlic to the bowl. Pour the curing solution over the meat and spices. If the meat floats, use a ceramic saucer or a small plate (do not use metal or wood) to weigh down the meat. Allow the meat to cure for 24 hours in the refrigerator.

Remove the meat from the refrigerator. Drain and discard the curing solution and spices. Place pork in a large pot, and cover with fresh water. Stud an onion with the cloves, and add to the pot. Bring pot to a boil, and allow to boil for 3 hours. During the last hour, add in the turnips and boil until easily pierced with a fork, and the meat is tender and pulling away from the bone. DO NOT ADD SALT, as the cure is salt based.

Remove meat from water and set aside. Discard onion. Remove turnips, and mash until smooth. Add a small amount of broth to the mashed turnips, if desired. Slice pork, and serve surrounded by the mashed turnips.

Serves 10

Cucumbers with Creamy Mint Dressing

5 cucumbers, peeled and sliced
1 cup sour cream
1/2 cup milk
1/2 cup mayonnaise
1 tbsp. sugar
3 tbsp. lemon juice
3 tbsp. vinegar
salt and pepper, to taste
20 mint leaves

Combine the sour cream, milk, mayonnaise, sugar, lemon juice, vinegar, salt and pepper in a blender. Blend until smooth. Add in the mint leaves, and blend until the mint is well chopped. Serve over sliced cucumbers. The dressing will thicken in the refrigerator.

Serves 6 - 8

Spiced Tea

- 4 tea bags
- 4 cups boiling water
- 3 limes
- 1 stick cinnamon
- 2 whole cloves
- 1/2 cup honey

For Hot Tea: Place tea bags and remaining ingredients in a teapot. Let the tea steep for 5 minutes. Remove tea bags. Stir to dissolve honey.

Makes 1 quart

For Iced Tea: Increase tea bags to 8. Pour boiling water over tea and remaining ingredients. Allow to steep for 5 minutes. Remove tea bags, and add 4 more cups of water. Allow to cool. Remove spices and limes, and serve over ice.

Makes 2 quarts

Apple Dumplings

Syrup:
1 1/2 cups sugar
2 cups water
1 tsp. ground cinnamon
1 whole cinnamon stick
1/2 tsp. nutmeg
pinch ground cardamom
pinch ground mace

Dumplings:
3 Granny Smith apples
juice of 1 lemon
2 1/4 cups flour
2 tsp. baking powder
2/3 cup shortening
1/2 cup milk

Sugar
cinnamon
2 tbsp. butter, cut into six pieces

- Combine syrup ingredients in a saucepan and place on stove. Allow to simmer for 3-4 minutes. Remove from heat.

- Peel and core apples. Cut in half, then cut each half in slices, keeping the sliced apple half intact. Place in a bowl with the lemon juice. Set aside. Heat oven to 375°.

- Sift together flour and baking powder. Knead in shortening until mixture resembles crumbs the size of peas. Add milk, and mix until you have a smooth dough. On a floured surface, roll out half of the dough into a rectangle. Cut the rectangle into 3 equal rectangles. Place sliced apple half in the center of one of the small rectangles . Sprinkle over 1 teaspoon sugar and a pinch of cinnamon. Top with a piece of butter. Cover the apple with one of the sides of the dough, then cover with the other side. Pinch edges to seal. Cut a slit in the top. Form the remaining dumplings in the same fashion.

- Place dumplings in a 9"x 13" glass baking dish. Pour syrup over the top. Bake for 45 minutes. Serve warm.

Makes 6 dumplings

Shrimp Stuffed Avocados

Shrimp Stuffed Avocados

Refresco Tropical
(Tropical Drink)

Blarney Stones

One of our stops on our honeymoon was to visit my husband's friend Lalo in Mexico City. After a brief stay in Cuernavaca, we headed for Lake Tequesquitengo, a small resort outside the Distrito Federal. It is a freshwater lake where water skiers strut their stuff. After a trying day of the sport, we sat down at waterside rest stop where we were served avocados stuffed with shrimp. If we had been in our right minds, we would have probably skipped over these mayonnaise rich little delicacies, in the Land of Dubious Refrigeration. Chalk it up to the carefree abandon of youth; we each ate about 3 of them. Maybe it was the amazing freshness of the shrimp, the tree ripeness of the avocados, or the haze of the late afternoon. I have never eaten any better.

The Blarney Stones were a favorite at my summer camp. They are perfect for lazy afternoons by the pool, or ladies teas. The flavor combination is a little unusual, but a refreshing change from the ordinary.

Serve with: sliced melon or fruit

Shrimp Stuffed Avocados

2 cups (1/2 lb) small shrimp, boiled, peeled, and deveined
    (equals 1 lb raw shrimp)
1/4 cup mayonnaise
1 tomato, seeded and chopped
1 - 2 tbsp. cilantro, chopped
salt and pepper to taste
4 ripe avocados

Mix together shrimp, mayonnaise, tomato, and cilantro. Add salt and pepper to taste. Store in refrigerator until ready to serve.

Right before serving, cut avocados in half, and remove pit. Fill hollow of avocado with shrimp mixture. Serve immediately with spoons.

Serves 4

Refresco Tropical

(Tropical Drink)

Milk of one coconut
3 tbsp. lime juice
1 banana
2 cups chopped pineapple
2 cups chopped papaya
water
sugar, if desired

Combine the ingredients in a blender, and puree, adding enough water to facilitate blending. Pour into pitcher. Add enough water to make 2 quarts. Add sugar, if needed.

Makes two quarts

Blarney Stones

- Cake:
- 4 eggs, separated, reserving 1 egg yolk for frosting
- 1 cup flour
- 1 1/2 tsp. baking powder
- 1/4 tsp. salt
- 1 cup sugar
- 1/2 cup boiling water
- 1/2 tsp. vanilla

- Frosting:
- 1 cup butter, softened
- 1 egg yolk (see above)
- 2 1/2 cups powdered sugar
- 1 tsp. vanilla
- 1/2 cup salted peanuts, chopped

Heat oven to 350°. Grease and flour a 9"x 13" baking pan. Combine flour, baking powder and salt in a bowl, and set aside. Beat three egg yolks until lemon colored. Add in sugar. Alternate adding in egg mixture to the dry ingredients with the boiling water. Add vanilla. In a separate bowl, beat the 4 remaining egg whites until stiff, then fold into batter. Pour into prepared pan, and bake for 30 minutes. Allow to cool completely before frosting.

To make frosting, cream together the softened butter and remaining egg yolk. Add in the powdered sugar and vanilla, beating well. Frost cake in pan, then sprinkle peanuts evenly over the top. Cut into squares and serve.

Serves 16 generously

Father's Day Breakfast

Huevos Rancheros
(Rancher Style Eggs)

Chilaquiles

Semitas Chorreadas
(Filled Semitas)

Mexican Hot Chocolate

The sauce for the *Huevos Rancheros* is a classic Mexican hot sauce. Serve it on the side. If you want a hotter sauce, add in a couple more chilies.

My husband requested the *chilaquiles* last Father's day. I think I ate most of them. They are great for a snack, or an easy late night meal.

Semitas are a traditional bread, but are difficult to find in bakeries. Finding a recipe for them proves difficult as well. These *semitas* take their inspiration from the ones I have eaten in Saltillo, Coahuila, Mexico.

The *piloncillo* filling will harden a bit when the semitas cool. Serve the *semitas* warmed up, so that the filling will be gooey.

Serve with: refried beans

Huevos Rancheros
(Rancher Style Eggs)

2 eggs per person

Fry the eggs, then serve with the hot sauce below.

Hot sauce:
3 tomatoes
3 serrano chilies
1 - 2 cloves garlic
pinch whole comino
pinch whole black pepper
salt

In a small saucepan, boil tomatoes and chilies in water for about 3 minutes. Remove tomatoes and peel. Remove chilies, and place in a *molcajete*, or in the container of a blender. Add in garlic, comino, pepper, and salt. Grind spices until you have a smooth paste (add enough liquid to the blender to facilitate blending). Add in tomatoes, and puree well. Salt to taste.

If you wish, you can cook this sauce to reduce the liquid. Add 1 tablespoons of oil to a skillet and heat. Add in sauce, and reduce until thickened.

Makes about 1 cup

Chilaquiles

12 tortillas
oil
1 28oz can tomatillos, drained
1 clove garlic
1 - 3 serrano chilies
salt to taste
1 onion, sliced
3/4 cup Mexican cream, or creme fraiche
1 cup queso fresco, feta cheese or monterrey jack cheese

Cut tortillas in quarters. Make tostadas either
by frying the tortillas in oil, or baking them in
a 350° oven leaving the oven door ajar, until
crispy and golden (see Basics).

Combine tomatillos, garlic, chile and salt in a
blender. Puree well. In a skillet, heat a small
amount of oil. Pour in sauce, add onion slices
and simmer until reduced, breaking onions
into rings.

In an oven proof dish, arrange tortilla quarters.
Pour sauce over, then cream, then cheese. Bake
in the oven at 350° until bubbling, about 15
minutes. Serve hot.

Serves 2 - 4

Semitas Chorreadas

(Filled Semitas)

Tea:
1 tsp. star anise
3 whole cloves
1/2 stick cinnamon
1 cup water

Semita:
1/2 cup tea
1/2 cup heavy cream
1/3 cup butter
4 1/2 - 5 cups flour
1 tsp. salt
2 pkgs yeast
1/2 cup sugar
2 eggs
2 tsp. anise seed (not star anise)

Filling:
2 8oz *piloncillos*
2/3 cup water
1 tsp. star anise
1 stick cinnamon
2 whole cloves
3/4 cup chopped pecans

- Boil tea ingredients for 3 - 5 minutes. Remove from heat. Make sure you end up with at least 1/2 cup of tea. Strain out spices.

- In a mixer bowl, add in 2 cups of the flour, salt, yeast and sugar. Affix dough kneading hooks to the mixer.

- Combine 1/2 cup tea, cream and butter in a saucepan. Allow the butter to melt. Heat or cool the liquid to 105°-115°. Add liquid to the flour mixture. Start mixer, and add in enough of the remaining flour to make a stiff dough. Add in eggs and anise seed. Knead dough for 10 minutes. Remove dough from mixer, and place in a greased bowl. Place bowl in a warm place, and allow to rise for 1 hour, or until doubled in bulk.

- Meanwhile, combine the filling ingredients except pecans in a saucepan. Begin to boil, and try to break up *piloncillo* (a potato masher helps). Boil filling until it reaches 230° on a candy thermometer. While the mixture is still hot, remove the spices with a slotted spoon, then add pecans. Stir well to distribute pecans.

- Pour the hot syrup onto a well greased pan. Mixture will crystalize as it cools. To use the filling, you need to break the cooled crystallized mixture into small chunks. You can also leave the *piloncillo* mixture cool in the same pan where was cooked, heating the pan when the mixture has cooled to release the hardened mixture. Break into pieces.

After dough has risen, punch down dough. Divide dough into 8 equal portions. Stretching the dough a bit, make a small cup, about 5" in diameter. Fill the cup with a few chunks of the filling. Gather the edges of the cup over the filling, and pinch to seal well. Make sure the dough is not too thin at the seams. Place seam side down on a greased baking sheet, and allow to rise in a warm place for about 1 hour, or until doubled in bulk.

Heat your oven to 350˚. Bake for 20 - 25 minutes, until golden brown.

Makes 8 semitas

# exican Hot Chocolate

- **1 cup milk**
- **1 oz Mexican chocolate**

Heat milk and chocolate together in a saucepan. When chocolate is melted, and the milk is well heated, beat well with a *molinillo*, or transfer the liquid to a blender to achieve a properly frothy mug of chocolate.

Serves 1

Mother's Day Breakfast

Maple Pecan Overnight Rolls

Orange Banana Juice

Strawberries with Rompope

If my kids could cook, this is what I would order for my Mother's Day breakfast. But since they can't, maybe I'll talk their dad into taking them fishing, and I'll make this for myself.

All of this can be done the night before. And if you don't have *rompope* on hand, just use powdered sugar, or maybe a little cream on your berries.

Maple Pecan Overnight Rolls

- **Syrup:**
- 1 cup maple syrup
- 1 stick butter
- 1 cup brown sugar
- 1/2 cup chopped pecans

- **Rolls:**
- 6 - 6 1/2 cups flour
- 1/3 cup sugar
- 2 pkg yeast
- 1 1/2 tsp. salt
- 3/4 cup warm water (105°-115°)
- 3/4 cup warm milk (105°-115°)
- 2 eggs
- 1 cup raisins
- 1 tbsp. cinnamon

In a 9"x 13" pan, heat maple syrup and butter. When butter is melted, remove from heat. Add brown sugar and pecans. Mix to distribute pecans evenly. Set aside.

In a mixer, combine 2 cups of flour, sugar, yeast and salt. Add in warm liquids, and begin to mix. When combined, add in eggs. Continue to mix, adding in enough of the remaining flour to make a firm, elastic dough. Allow mixer to knead dough (using the dough hook attachment) for about 8 minutes.

On a floured surface, roll out dough into a long rectangle, about 1/4" thick. Distribute raisins and cinnamon evenly over the surface of the rectangle. Starting on one of the long sides of the rectangle, roll the rectangle into a cylinder. Seal the edge. Cut into about 20 slices. Place slices in the prepared syrup pan. Cover with plastic, and store in the refrigerator overnight. (Rolls will have completely risen in 2-24 hours.)

Heat oven to 375°. Remove rolls from refrigerator, and remove plastic. Place pan in preheated oven. Bake for 30-35 minutes. To serve, invert pan of rolls onto large platter, drizzling the remaining syrup over the top over the rolls.

Makes about 20 rolls

 # trawberries with Rompope

2 pints strawberries, washed and hulled
***rompope* (recipe, page 131)**
mint sprigs or lime zest (optional)

Slice strawberries into four separate bowls. Serve with two or three tablespoons of rompope drizzled over the top. Garnish with mint or lime zest, if desired.

Serves 4

 # range Banana Juice

- **1 quart orange juice**
- **1 banana**

Combine ingredients in blender. Puree well. Serve chilled.

Serves 4

Tacos de Mollejas

Tacos de Mollejas
(Beef Sweetbread Tacos)

Hongos con Chile Dulce
(Mushrooms with Sweet Peppers)

Orange Cupcakes

Sweet breads are very inexpensive in the store these days, although they often appear on the menu in very posh restaurants. To use a cliché, they taste a bit like chicken, even though they are beef. Serve the *mollejas* with a nice salsa and some hot corn tortillas.

I love mushrooms, and am always thinking of how to work them into a dish. I also like the idea of the mushrooms <u>being</u> the dish. Mushrooms shrink a bit when cooked, therefore this recipe calls for quite a few. The mushrooms also make great *taquitos*, a nice meal to offer to vegetarians.

Cupcakes remind me of Lydia, my sister-in-law. She is always ready to crash kiddie parties in search of cupcakes. The Orange Cupcakes are great for any occasion. Since they have no frosting, and have a natural orange flavor and color, they aren't too decadent. That way, Lydia can have a few more.

Serve with: beans, rice, tortillas, salsa, cold beer

Tacos de Mollejas

(Beef Sweetbread Tacos)

3 lbs *mollejas* (beef sweetbreads)
salt to taste
2 - 3 tbsp. oil

In a large pot, boil *mollejas* in salted water for one hour. Remove from water, and let cool. Cut *mollejas* into bite-sized pieces, removing any membranes.

In a skillet, heat oil. Add in cut up *mollejas*. Brown *mollejas* until golden. Serve with hot tortillas and your favorite salsa or *pico de gallo*.

Serves 6

Hongos con Chile Dulce

(Mushrooms with Sweet Peppers)

1/4 - 1/2 cup olive oil
1 onion, sliced
1/2 red bell pepper, seeded and chopped
1/2 yellow bell pepper, seeded and chopped
1/2 green bell pepper, seeded and chopped
2 cloves garlic, minced
3 lbs fresh mushrooms, washed
salt to taste

In a large pot, saute the onion in the olive oil. When the onion is translucent, add in the peppers. Saute the peppers for 5 minutes. Add mushrooms and garlic. Cover, and allow to simmer for about 10 minutes. Serve warm.

Serves 6

Orange Cupcakes

- 1 cup sugar
- 1/2 cup butter, softened
- 2 eggs
- 1 1/2 cups cake flour
- 1 1/2 tsp. baking powder
- 1/2 cup orange juice
- 1 tbsp. grated orange peel
- powdered sugar

Heat oven to 350°. Cream together sugar and butter in a bowl. Add in eggs. Sift in flour and baking powder. Add in orange juice and peel. Pour into paper lined or greased muffin tins. Bake for 25 minutes, or until a toothpick comes out clean from center cake. Sift powdered sugar over the top while cooling. (Reduce baking time to 20 minutes if making mini cupcakes.)

Makes 1 dozen cupcakes, or 32 mini cupcakes

Liver and Onions

Liver and Onions
Spinach with Cheese and Tomatoes
Jalapeño Corn Bread
Ice Cream Pie

Mom is a liver lover. I am not sure how many of them are in existence, but if you put them all in a parade, she'd probably be waving their banner. Her mother made liver as described below. Adding in water to steam the liver makes it tender.

L iver and Onions

- 6 strips of bacon
- 3 onions, sliced into rings
- 2 1/2 lbs fresh calves liver, sliced
- flour (about 2 cups)
- salt and pepper
- 2 tbsp. water

Fry the bacon in a large lidded skillet, until the fat renders and bacon is crisp. Remove the bacon, and set aside for another use (see spinach recipe). Add onions to the skillet, and cook until translucent. Remove and set aside.

Season the flour with salt and pepper. Dredge liver in the flour, and place in the heated skillet. Brown the liver on both sides, about 3 minutes on each side. Fry all the liver, removing any cooked slices to accommodate uncooked slices. When all the liver is cooked, return it all to the pan, with onions, and add the water. Cover the skillet with the lid, and allow liver and onions to steam for about 3-4 minutes.

Serves 6

Spinach with Cheese and Tomatoes

1 lb spinach, washed well
3 tbsp. butter
1/3 cup flour
1 cup milk
1 cup grated cheese
salt to taste
pinch cayenne pepper
1 cup tomatoes, chopped and seeded
crumbled bacon (optional)

In a lidded saucepan, steam spinach in a small amount of water, about 4 minutes. Drain well, and set aside.

In another saucepan, melt butter. Add in flour, and mix until all the flour is absorbed. Add in milk. Stir until the sauce is thickened. Stir in cheese; cook until cheese is melted. Season with salt and cayenne pepper. Add in the cooked spinach. Pour into a serving dish, and sprinkle top with chopped tomatoes. Top with crumbled bacon, if desired.

Serves 6

Jalapeño Cornbread

- 1 cup flour
- 1 cup cornmeal
- 1 tbsp. baking powder
- 1 tsp. salt
- 1/2 tsp. baking soda
- 1 cup sour cream
- 1 cup milk
- 1 egg
- 1/4 cup oil
- 1/3 cup pickled jalapeños, chopped

Grease and flour a 8"x 8" baking pan. Heat your oven to 450°. Sift together flour, cornmeal, baking powder, salt, and soda. In a separate bowl, beat together the sour cream, milk, egg and oil. Add in the flour mixture a bit at a time to the milk, mixing well after each addition. Add in the jalapeños, and mix to distribute well. Pour batter into prepared pan, and bake for 20 minutes, until golden brown.

Serves 6 - 8

I ce Cream Pie

22 chocolate sandwich cookies

1/4 cup butter, melted

1 quart of your favorite flavor of ice cream

1/3 cup heavy cream

2 tbsp. corn syrup

4 oz semisweet chocolate, chopped

Finely grind cookies with melted butter in a food processor until moist clumps form. Press crumbs into a 9" pie plate. Freeze 15 minutes. Take ice cream out of freezer and allow to soften.

Spoon ice cream into crust, mounding in center. Freeze until ice cream is firm, about 30 minutes.

Combine cream and corn syrup in a heavy small saucepan. Bring to simmer over medium heat, whisking constantly. Remove from heat. Add chocolate and whisk until melted and smooth. Cool to barely lukewarm, whisking occasionally, about 20 minutes. Spoon over ice cream, covering completely. Freeze until firm, about 30 minutes. Can be made 2 days in advance.

Serves 8

Caldo de Res

Caldo de Res
(Beef Soup)
Chilled Guava Cream

You really don't need a recipe to make a Mexican style beef soup. The basic requirements are that you use whole green chiles in the stock, along with tomatoes, garlic, onions, salt and pepper. When you make the soup, you can add in whatever vegetables you have on hand. Corn on the cob is a favorite, as well as cabbage. You might want to add a little cilantro. If you want to put in some noodles, I suggest *fideo* (vermicelli noodles). In a skillet, heat about 2 tablespoons of oil. Brown a 5oz package of *fideo* until golden, then add to the soup pot. If you brown the *fideo*, you don't have to worry about your noodles turning to mush. Browning the noodles keeps them firm, even if the soup is reheated several times.

You can serve chopped chilies, or shredded cheese as a topping.

Serve with: corn tortillas or tostadas

Caldo de Res
(Beef Soup)

Stock:
4 lbs beef with bones
1 onion, peeled
2 whole tomatoes
2 cloves garlic, peeled
2 whole serrano chilies
salt to taste

Soup:
3 cloves garlic
pinch whole comino
1/4 tsp. whole pepper
3 tomatoes

Soup vegetables:
3 whole serrano chilies
4 carrots, chopped
3 ribs celery, chopped
12 - 15 new potatoes, halved
1/2 head cabbage, chopped
3 ears corn, cut into 3 pieces each
3 - 4 zucchini, chopped

In a 6 quart stock pot, add beef, onion, tomatoes, garlic, chilies, and salt. Cover with water. Bring to a boil, and simmer for about 1 1/2 hours. Skim foam off of surface. Remove beef, cut meat from bone and cut into bite sized pieces. Remove vegetables and discard. Return bone and meat to the pot.

In a *molcajete*, or with a mortar and pestle, grind the garlic with the whole comino and pepper. Add to stock pot. In a blender, puree tomatoes, using a little beef broth to facilitate blending. Add to the pot.

Add in fresh vegetables, and simmer for another 20 minutes.

Serves 12

Chilled Guava Cream

2 12oz cans guava nectar (3 cups total)
3 envelopes unflavored gelatin
3/4 cup sugar
2 cups yogurt
1 cup sour cream
a colorful garnish, such as strawberries,
    mint leaves, or non-pareils

Pour unflavored gelatin into a bowl. In a saucepan, bring to a boil 1 1/2 cups of the guava nectar. Pour boiling nectar over the gelatin. Stir for 2 minutes, until gelatin is dissolved. Add in remaining ingredients, beating with an electric hand mixer until smooth. Pour into a six cup mold, or into 12 individual 1/2 cup molds. Chill until firm. Garnish as desired.

Serves 12

Fried Chicken

Fried Chicken with Cream Gravy

Buttermilk Biscuits

Watercress and Melon Salad

Custard Pie

Fried chicken is the manna of the Southern United States. (How wonderful if it fell from the sky!) Every family cooks it differently than the next, but yours is always the best. Frying chicken is not as easy as it seems. The outside coating may brown faster than the meat cooks. Fry your chicken slowly, but not so slow that it becomes greasy.

This is a mammoth recipe for biscuits, but I like putting them away in the freezer for later. If you don't want this many biscuits, just cut the recipe proportions in half.

Serve with: mashed potatoes

 # ried Chicken with Cream Gravy

Chicken:
shortening for frying
2 cups buttermilk
1 egg
2 cups flour
salt and pepper
1 3 lb chicken, cut into pieces

Cream gravy:
1/2 cup flour (use leftover dredging flour)
1 quart milk
salt
freshly cracked black pepper

Melt 2-3 cups of shortening in a large frying pan. Beat together buttermilk and egg in a shallow dish. On a separate plate, combine flour, salt and pepper. Dip chicken a few times in the buttermilk, then dredge in the flour. Place chicken piece in the hot oil, and fry over a low flame for 20-30 minutes.

For the gravy, drain oil from skillet, leaving 3 tablespoons of drippings, plus the browned bits of chicken and coating mixture. Scrape up any bits stuck to the skillet. Return skillet to a low flame. Add in 1/2 cup flour, and mix with drippings. When well combined add in 1 quart of milk, and salt and pepper. Stir until thickened and bubbling. Serve with mashed potatoes.

Serves 4

Watercress and Melon Salad

1 melon, either honeydew or cantaloupe
1 bunch watercress, torn into bite sized pieces
Poppyseed Dressing (see recipe below)

Cut the melon in half, and scoop out seeds. Using a melon baller, cut melon into bite sized balls. Toss together with water cress. Top with about 1/3 cup poppyseed dressing.

Serves 4

Poppyseed Dressing

- 1 onion, peeled and quartered
- 1/4 cup dijon mustard
- 3/4 cup apple cider vinegar
- 2/3 cup honey
- 1 cup salad oil
- 1 tsp. salt
- 3 tbsp. poppy seeds

Combine onion, mustard, cider vinegar, and honey in a blender. Puree until smooth. Through the hole in the top, drizzle the oil slowly into the vortex of the pureeing mixture. Stop blender, and stir in salt and poppy seeds. Store in the refrigerator.

Makes 2 1/2 cups

 **uttermilk Biscuits**

5 cups flour
2 1/2 tbsp. baking powder
1 heaping tbsp. sugar
1 tsp. salt
1 cup shortening
3/4 to 1 cup buttermilk

Heat oven to 450°. Mix together flour, baking powder, sugar, salt and shortening, combining until it resembles coarse meal. Add in buttermilk, just enough to make a stiff but elastic dough.

On a floured surface, knead dough for 1-2 minutes, incorporating flour to make the dough less sticky. Roll out to 1/2 to 3/4 inch thickness, and cut with biscuit cutter or drinking glass rim, 2 1/2 inches in diameter. Place biscuits on an ungreased cookie sheet, and bake for 10-12 minutes, until golden brown.

Makes 24 - 30 biscuits

 **ustard Pie**

- Pastry for a 9" pie shell (see Basics)
-
- 4 eggs
- 3 egg yolks
- 3/4 cup sugar
- 2 1/2 cups milk
- 1 tsp. vanilla
  pinch salt
  ground nutmeg
-
- Heat your oven to 350°. Roll out pastry for pie shell. Line pie plate with pastry. Bake for 5-7 minutes, until slightly firm. Set aside.

- Combine the eggs, yolks, sugar, milk, vanilla and salt. Whisk until smooth. Pour into prepared pastry. Sprinkle nutmeg on the **top. Bake for 30 minutes.**

- With two strips of aluminum foil, fashion a collar for the pie to prevent the crust from over browning. Place around the pie after 30 minutes of baking. Bake for 25-30 minutes more, or until a knife comes clean out of the edge of the filling (55 to 60 minutes total baking time). The center will puff up, but will set and become firm while cooling.
  Cool completely before serving.

Serves 8

Milanesa de Ternera

Milanesa de Ternera
(Veal Cutlets)

Minty peas

Tepache
(Pineapple Wine)

Polocotes
(Nut and Jam Cookies)

Milanesa is a term for meat that is cooked in the Milan style, therefore, not too different from a veal cutlet you would get in an Italian restaurant. You don't have to use veal; beef, chicken or pork scallops would work just as well as long as the meat is thin. The breading on *Milanesa* is never heavy, and does not use eggs. I have never seen it with a sauce either, but I think this light glaze finishes the dish nicely.

Tepache is a refreshing home brew that uses the discarded bits of a pineapple. Like making lemonade, you need to taste your drink, and adjust the water and sugar to your liking.

Polocotes are my invention. *Polocote* is, well, for lack of a more fitting word, a weed. It grows locally, is bright yellow, and is sometimes the only glimpse of color seen on our parched plains. *Polocote* looks like sunflowers, and a bit like these cookies. Thus, the name.

Serve with: hot french rolls

ilanesa de Ternera

(Veal Cutlets)

1 1/2 lbs veal scalloppini
1/2 cup flour
1 tbsp. fresh thyme leaves, or 1 1/2 tsp. dried thyme
1/2 cup olive oil
salt and pepper

Sauce:
2/3 cup chicken broth
1/3 cup dry sherry
1 tbsp. fresh lemon juice
1 clove garlic, minced

Pound veal with a tenderizing hammer to 1/8 inch thickness. Sprinkle with salt and pepper. Mix flour and 2 1/2 teaspoon fresh thyme (or 1 teaspoon dried thyme) in
shallow dish. Dredge veal in flour mixture, shaking off excess. Heat 1/4 cup olive oil in large skillet over medium heat. Add veal, pan fry until veal begins to brown, about 1 minute per side. Place on platter. Repeat with remaining 1/4 cup of oil and remaining veal.

After veal is cooked, remove to a plate and keep warm. In the same skillet, add broth, sherry, lemon juice and garlic, and bring to a boil, scraping up browned bits. Add remaining fresh or dried thyme. Simmer until sauce thickens slightly, about 3 minutes. Season sauce with salt and pepper. Serve veal on a platter with the sauce poured over, or on the side.

Serves 4

inty Peas

1 cup water
1 lb fresh peas, shelled, or 1 16 oz bag frozen peas
10 mint leaves
Mint leaves for garnish

Stove top cooking: Boil 1 cup of water in a saucepan. Add in peas and mint leaves. Cover, and steam for 5 minutes. Remove from heat. Remove mint leaves before serving, and garnish with fresh mint leaves.

Microwave cooking: In a small microwaveable dish, place peas. Lay mint leaves over peas. Cover dish with plastic wrap, and microwave on high for about 4 minutes. Remove plastic wrap and mint leaves right before serving. Garnish with fresh mint leaves.

Serves 4 - 6

Tepache

(Pineapple Wine)

1 pineapple rind, washed,
    and any left over pineapple bits or core (not leaves)
1 quart water
1 *piloncillo* (8 oz)
up to 1 quart water

Place pineapple rind and core in a 1 quart
glass or ceramic container. Pour in water, and
let ferment for 72 hours. Filter liquid into a
pitcher, and discard pineapple remains. Add
in *piloncillo*, and let dissolve. You may want
to dilute drink with up to 1 quart of water.
Tepache should have a distinct wine flavor.

Makes 2 quarts

Polocotes

(Nut and Jam Cookies)

- 2/3 cup butter, softened
- 1/2 cup sugar
- 1 1/2 cups flour
- 1/4 tsp. salt
- 2 eggs, separated
- 1 tsp. vanilla
- 3 - 4 drops yellow food coloring (optional)
- 1 1/2 cups pecans, very finely chopped
- peach or pineapple jam

Heat your oven to 350°. Cream together the
sugar and butter. Sift in the flour and salt. Add
in the egg yolks, vanilla and coloring. Mix until
you have a firm dough. Divide the dough into 4
equal portions, then divide each portion into
twelve pieces. Roll the pieces into balls.
Continue shaping until all the dough has been
formed into balls.

Place egg whites in a shallow dish, and pour
chopped pecans onto a plate. Dip each ball into
the egg white, then roll in the chopped pecans.
Place on an ungreased cookie sheet. When all
the dough balls have been prepared in this fashion, press your thumb onto each dough ball to
make an indentation. Fill the indentation with
1/2 teaspoon of jam. Bake cookies for 15-18
minutes, until brown.

Makes 4 dozen cookies

Seafood Fry

Seafood fry and French Fries with Beer Batter

Border Buttermilk

Raspberry Mousse

This menu is really fun if you are having a bunch of people over, and you'd like to do something outdoors. We tried this recipe in one of my couples cooking classes. The men were in charge of the frying. First, they discarded the recipe. Then, they poured the entirety of the battered shrimp into the frying kettle, which resulted in a fried shrimp loaf, rather than individual fried shrimp. Then, the moths got interested in the butane flame under the frying kettle. The moths were in search of light, but ended up zooming into the hot grease.

In spite of everything, the shrimp were consumed completely, which goes to show that good company and fun times are the best of seasonings.

Serve with: seafood sauces, salad, french bread

Seafood Fry and French Fries with Beer Batter

This is one of those recipes that can only be described, not listed. Fish, shrimp and oysters are the standard frying fare, but you may want to throw in some squid, octopus or clams for variety. Ask your seafood vendor what they have that is extremely fresh, and buy that. By the way, make sure you remove the oysters, shrimp, and clams from their shell before frying. Make sure your potatoes are very fresh, because soggy potatoes cannot make crisp fries. For every 3 pounds of seafood and potatoes, you will need the following amount of batter:

1 cup flour
1/3 cup cornstarch
salt and pepper
2 cups beer

Combine the batter ingredients in a shallow casserole dish (casseroles are great for batter dipping and flour dredging). Coat each piece of seafood well, and place in the hot oil. Fry 2-4 minutes for shrimp, oysters, and clams, and 7-10 minutes for fish.

Use a good frying oil, such as corn oil. Peanut oil gives a great nutty flavor to your seafood, so try that sometime. Your oil should be heated to 375° for quick frying without burning. You can either fry indoors, or outdoors, over a butane flame. But please, **MAKE SURE THE KIDS ARE IN A SAFE LOCATION ANY TIME YOU FRY FOOD, ESPECIALLY OUTDOORS**.

If you are frying your fish in the kitchen in a skillet, fry each side of the fish for 4-5 minutes. If you are frying in a deep fryer outside, remember that the wind will carry off a lot of the heat, so frying will take longer. Since I cannot predict what your weather conditions will be, I can't tell you how long it will take to cook your fish.

The french fries are prepared the same way as the seafood. Russet potatoes are a good french fry choice. Dip the matchstick sized potatoes slices in the batter, after you cook the seafood, and add to the hot oil. Fry until golden.

The potatoes will be crispier if you soak them for 20 minutes in iced water before cooking. Drain the water, dry them a bit with a paper towel, then proceed with the dipping and frying.

aspberry Mousse

1 envelope unflavored gelatin
1/4 cup water
3/4 lb fresh raspberries
1 cup milk
1 cup sugar
1 pint heavy cream
extra raspberries
mint leaves
whipped cream

Place gelatin in a bowl. Sprinkle water over gelatin, and allow gelatin to dissolve completely.

Wash raspberries. Place raspberries in a blender container with the milk and sugar. Puree well. Press puree through a wire sieve to extract any raspberry seeds. Discard seeds. Fold in dissolved gelatin.

In a separate bowl, whip the cream until stiff peaks form. Fold in raspberry mixture. Pour into a six cup mold, or into individual serving glasses. Chill until firm. Garnish with extra raspberries, mint leaves and whipped cream.

Serves 8

order Buttermilk

- 1/4 cup fresh lime juice
- 1 cup fresh pineapple or 1 cup pineapple juice
- 1/4 cup maraschino cherry syrup
- 1 cup tequila
- 1/3 cup sugar
- 6 - 10 cups ice

Puree all the ingredients in a blender, adding in the amount of ice needed to make a slush. Serve immediately.

Serves 8

169

Caldo Gallego

Caldo Gallego

Molletes

Orange Flan

Caldo Gallego is a traditional soup from Galicia, a province in Spain. It is a hearty soup, wonderful on a cold winter's night. If you happen to have a freezer full of sausage, now is your chance to use it.

Molletes are a traditional Mexican snack, that go well with simple meals. And, I am quite fond of the Orange Flan. It is much more delicate than the *Flan de Cafe*, and has the refreshing nuance of orange flavor. If you can find them, garnish your flan with orange leaves and orange blossoms. If you want a plain flan, just omit the orange extract and add 1/2 teaspoon more of vanilla.

Caldo Gallego

- 1 cup dried navy beans, picked over
- 2 1/2 quarts water
- 1 onion, chopped
- 2 oz salt pork, rind removed
- 1/2 lb ham, in cubes (serrano ham, if possible)
- 1 - 2 bay leaves
- 1 sprig fresh thyme, or 1/4 tsp. dried thyme
- 2 large turnips or potatoes, peeled and diced
- 1 - 1 1/4 lbs venison sausage, or your favorite link sausage
- 6 oz Mexican chorizo
- 1 bunch turnip greens (4 - 5 cups chopped)

Boil water in large pot. Add beans, and boil rapidly for two minutes. Take off heat, and let stand for 1 hour.

Return beans to heat. Add onion, salt pork, ham, bay leaves, and thyme. Boil for 1 1/2 hours. Add more water, if necessary. Add turnips. Leaving their casings on, add sausage and chorizo. Boil for 30 more minutes. During the last 10 minutes, add turnip greens. After boiling time has finished, turn off heat, and prick sausage and chorizo to drain juices into the soup. Remove sausage and chorizo, and carefully peel off casings. Slice sausage and chorizo into rounds, and return to pot. Serve immediately (Avoid stirring too much after this point, so sausage and chorizo slices will remain intact.)

Serves 6 - 8

 **olletes**

3 French bread rolls
butter
1 cup refried beans
1 cup grated white cheese, such as Monterrey Jack or asadero

Heat the broiler in your oven. Cut the rolls in
half lengthwise. Spread with butter, and toast
under the broiler until golden. Remove from
oven, and cool slightly. Spread with the refried
beans, then sprinkle with the grated cheese.
Return to the broiler to melt the cheese.
Serve hot.

Serves 6

Orange Flan

Caramel:
1/2 cup sugar
5 drops lemon juice
1/4 cup water

Flan:
1 quart milk
1 cup sugar
6 eggs
4 egg yolks
1/2 tsp. vanilla
1 tsp. orange extract

In a saucepan, combine the water, sugar and lemon juice. Bring to a boil, and simmer until the syrup turns dark. Pour into a 10" glass pie plate, spreading to cover as much of the bottom of the plate as possible. Set aside.

Fill a pitcher with water. Set aside. Find a baking pan in which your pie plate will fit. Set aside. Heat your oven to 325°.

In a large pot, bring milk and 1/2 cup sugar to a boil. Remove from heat. In a separate bowl, beat eggs, egg yolks, and remaining sugar with an electric hand mixer. One spoonful at a time, add in 2 cups of the hot milk while continuously beating the eggs. Pour egg mixture back into the pot of hot milk. Stir to break up any foam. Add in vanilla and orange extract. Pour flan mixture into a large empty pitcher.

Place the baking pan in the oven. Using pitcher, fill the pan with 1" of water. Place prepared pie plate in the baking pan with the water. Fill the pie plate with the flan mixture. Close the oven, and bake the flan for 50 minutes, until a knife comes clean out of the center. Cool. Invert onto a platter before serving. (Can also be made in individual custard cups. Reduce cooking time to 35 minutes.)

Serves 12

Enchiladas Rojas

Enchiladas Rojas
(Red Enchiladas)

Guisado de Elote y Calabasa
(Stewed Squash and Corn)

Horchata
(Rice Refreshment)

These *enchiladas* are different than what one usually finds in restaurants. They are not drowning in sauce, nor smothered with cheese. In fact, if you leave the cheese out of this recipe, you have a low fat, yet satisfying meal. The method described below is a more traditional technique of assembling *enchiladas*, dipping the tortillas in sauce, rather than pouring the sauce over the rolled tortillas.

Horchata is a drink made from boiled rice. It is a wonderful drink to give to babies, especially those who may have an upset tummy. For grown-ups, it is a nice change from soda, and remarkably refreshing.

Enchiladas Rojas

(Red Enchiladas)

- 1 chicken, boiled, deboned, skin removed, and shredded
- 4 dozen corn tortillas
- 12 oz queso fresco, crumbled or Monterrey Jack, grated
- 1 onion, chopped

Sauce:
- 1 lb tomatoes
- 5 dried ancho chilies
- 1/2 cup water
- 2 cloves garlic, peeled
- 2 tbsp. oil
- salt to taste

For the sauce, boil tomatoes and chilies until tender, about 10 minutes. Drain water, and add tomatoes and chilies to a blender container. Add in water and garlic, and puree well. Heat oil in a skillet. When hot, add in sauce, and simmer for about 10 minutes. Remove from heat, and set aside.

Dip tortillas in the sauce, lightly coating both sides completely. Place tortilla in a casserole dish, and add about 1 tablespoon of chicken to the tortilla. Roll up tortilla. Place at one end of the casserole dish. Proceed with the remaining tortillas in the same fashion. An extra casserole dish may be needed. When finished with the tortillas, sprinkle the onions over the top.

Sprinkle crumbled queso fresco over the top and serve (or, if using Monterrey Jack cheese, place casserole under a heated broiler to melt cheese before serving).

Serves 8

 # uisado de Elote y Calabasa

(Stewed Squash and Corn)

3 tbsp. oil
1 onion, chopped
2 cloves garlic, minced
1 1/2 lbs tatuma squash, cut into 1/2 inch cubes
2 ears corn, kernels cut off
salt
pepper
1/2 cup water

Heat oil in a large covered frying pan. Add in onions and garlic, and saute until onion is translucent. Add in squash and corn, stirring to coat with oil. Add salt and pepper to taste. When all the vegetables are well coated, add in the water. Place lid on pan, and allow to simmer for 20 minutes.

Serves 8

 # orchata

(Rice Refreshment)

8 cups water
1 cup rice
2 cinnamon sticks
1 cup of sugar (or to taste)
1 tbsp. ground cinnamon
water

In a saucepan, bring water, rice, and cinnamon sticks to a boil. Cook for 30 minutes, until rice is tender. Cool.

Remove cinnamon sticks. Place rice and liquid in the container of a blender (you may have to do a couple of batches). Puree well. Pour puree into a pitcher. Stir in sugar, ground cinnamon, and enough water to make 3 quarts of horchata. Chill well, and serve over ice.

Makes 3 quarts

Crepas de Huitlacoche

Crepas de Huitlacoche

Avocado and Bacon Salad

Orange Sherbet
(Purchased)

Huitlacoche (also known as Cuitlacoche) is a mushroom that grows on healthy ears of corn. It is difficult to propagate, needing very specific micro-climates to grow. It is prized as a delicacy in Mexico. I remember a story a few years back that someone found it growing in their crop here in the States. They thought it was the end of the corn world. But since this fungus is so particular about where it grows, it proved not to be a threat, but a treat. You can find it in cans in gourmet shops.

The dressing for the salad in this menu is the same found on the Orange Almond Salad. It is quite a versatile dressing that can go from sweet salads to savory salads.

- Crêpes:
- 1 tbsp. butter, melted
- 2 cups milk
- 1 egg, beaten
- 1 1/2 cups flour

- Filling:
- 2 tbsp. oil
- 1/2 onion, chopped
- 20 epazote leaves
- 2 8oz cans huitlacoche

- Sauce:
- 1/2 cup wine
- 1 shallot, peeled and chopped
- 10 - 15 epazote leaves
- 3 egg yolks
- 1 tbsp. lemon juice
- 1/2 cup butter
- 1 clove garlic, minced
- pinch salt
- dash white pepper

- Epazote leaves, for garnish

To make the crêpes: Beat together the butter and milk. Whisk in egg. Sift flour into milk mixture at bit at a time, whisking to mix. Try to break up any lumps, however, a few lumps are okay.

Heat a shallow teflon pan, or a crêpe pan. Pour in about 1/3 cup of the batter, swirling the pan so that the bottom has a thin layer of the batter. Return to the heat for 60 seconds. Flip crêpe, and cook on other side for 60 seconds. Remove crepe to a plate, and continue making crêpes in this fashion. One recipe of batter makes 8-9 crêpes.

To make the filling: Heat oil in a clean skillet. Add in onion and epazote, and fry until onion is translucent. Add in *huitlacoche*, and sauté for about 10 minutes. Set aside.

To make sauce: In a saucepan, place the wine, shallot and epazote leaves. Bring to a boil, and reduce until you have 1 - 2 tablespoons of liquid. Strain out and discard shallots and epazote leaves. Set aside the reduced liquid.

In another saucepan, whisk together the lemon juice and eggs yolks. Add in 1/4 cup of the butter. Heat the pan to just melt the butter. When completely melted, remove from heat. DO NOT COOK SAUCE!! Add in remaining butter, salt, pepper, garlic, and the reduced liquid. Whisk until all the butter is melted.

To make crepes: Heat your oven to 300°. Fill each crepe with 2 tablespoons of huitlacoche filling. Roll up and place in an oven proof casserole dish. When all the crêpes are filled, place dish in the heated oven for 10 minutes, until the crêpes are warm. Spoon the sauce over, then serve immediately. Garnish with epazote leaves.

Serves 2 - 4

Avocado and Bacon Salad

2 ripe avocados
1 head Boston Bibb lettuce, washed and separated into leaves
6 strips bacon, fried until crisp, and crumbled

Dressing:
3 tbsp. heavy cream
1/2 cup olive oil
1 tsp. sugar
2 scallions, chopped
1/2 tsp. dried or fresh dill
salt
pepper
1/4 cup white wine vinegar

Peel and slice avocados. Make a nest of the lettuce leaves on a platter. Arrange avocado slices on the lettuce, and sprinkle the crumbled bacon over.

Whisk together the cream, oil, sugar, scallions, dill, salt and pepper. When well combined, add in the vinegar, whisking until homogenous. Pour over avocados and serve immediately.

Serves 4

Herbed Chicken and Dumplings

Herbed Chicken and Dumplings

Stewed Eggplant and Tomatoes

Peach Cobbler

My grandmother always tried to make dumplings, but she never had any luck. Therefore, I have no secret family recipe to pass on to you. I remember her standing over a pot, staring at a sad mess, and shaking her head. I vaguely remember Grandaddy being around, but he knew better than to say anything. So I researched this recipe with my dumpling making friends, Ruby and Josie. They gave me lots of pointers and advice, so I have to give them credit for this recipe.

It is crucial that no one gets curious and checks the dumplings while they are cooking. Hands off that pot lid until the 15 minutes is up. Using milk in the dumplings make them fluffy, and whitens the chicken broth. Using the broth for the dumplings will give you a firm, smooth dumpling. Make sure your dumplings are very thin.

Herbed Chicken and Dumplings

Chicken:
1 chicken, cut into pieces
2 carrots
1 rib celery
1 clove garlic, peeled
2 tbsp. chopped parsley (or 2 tsp.dried)
2 tbsp. fresh thyme (or 2 tsp.dried)
1 onion, chopped
salt
pepper
water

Dumplings:
1 1/2 cups flour
2 tsp. baking powder
1 tsp. dill
pinch of salt
3 tbsp. shortening
1/3 cup milk or chicken broth

In a large stew pot, add in all the ingredients for the chicken. Cover the chicken with water. Bring to a boil, then simmer chicken until cooked, about 45 minutes. Remove from heat, then remove chicken from broth. Cool the chicken, then remove the meat from the bones. Return the chicken meat to the pot of broth.

For the dumplings, mix together flour, baking powder, dill, and salt. Knead in the shortening with your hands. When the flour and shortening are well combined, add in the milk or broth. Continue to mix the dough with your hands until the dough is somewhat stiff.

Return the pot of chicken to a boil. On a floured surface, roll out the dumplings to 1/8" thickness. Cut into 2" x 2" squares. Drop dumplings one by one into the boiling broth. Cover, and boil gently for 15 minutes. Do not remove lid until the 15 minutes are up and the dumplings have cooked.

Serves 4

S tewed Eggplant and Tomatoes

1 small onion, chopped
1/4 cup olive oil
1 eggplant, peeled and cubed
2 cloves garlic, minced
2 - 3 tomatoes, peeled and chopped
1 cup water
salt to taste
1 sprig fresh oregano, or 1 tsp.dried

In a covered skillet, saute onion in the oil until translucent. Add in eggplant, garlic and tomatoes, and saute until all the oil has been absorbed. Add in water, salt and oregano. Place lid on skillet, and allow eggplant to simmer for 20 minutes, until the eggplant is translucent.

Serves 4

P each Cobbler

- **Filling:**
- 5 - 6 cups of fresh peaches, peeled and sliced
- 1/2 cup sugar
- pinch cinnamon
- pinch ground mace
- pinch ground cardamom
-
- **Topping:**
- 1/4 cup butter
- 1/4 cup sugar
- 1 cup flour
- 1/4 cup milk
- 1 1/2 tsp. baking powder
- 1 egg
- 1/4 tsp. salt

Heat oven to 400°. In an oven proof dish, mix together the peaches, sugar and spices. For the topping, cream together the sugar and butter. Add in the remaining ingredients. Mix well. Pour over the top of the prepared fruit. Bake for 20 minutes. Serve warm.

Serves 6 - 8

Grilled Filet Mignon

Grilled Filet Mignon
Spaghetti with Chipotle Pecan Pesto
Spiced Pears in Syrup

Sometimes, you just need to eat a good steak. At your meat market, ask your butcher to help you select the finest filets available. Make sure there is sufficient marbling, and buy U.S.D.A prime aged beef, if available.

The Chipotle Pecan Pesto is great for traveling, on picnics, or to take to covered dish suppers. You can change the shape of the pasta from spaghetti to practically anything (I like orzo.)

Once a year, I will buy pears when they are inexpensive, and make the Spiced Pears in Syrup. We made these in one of my cooking classes. The participants were surprised by the refreshing flavor of the pears, and were equally impressed as to how easy they were to prepare. I can mine in canning jars. It is nice to have something homemade to serve when guests drop in. And, they make great gifts. Canning, however, is not necessary. The pears will keep a few weeks in your refrigerator.

 rilled Filet Mignon

- 4 6oz filet mignon rounds
- 4 strips bacon
- freshly cracked black pepper
- salt

Wrap bacon around the outside of the filet. Use a skewer to affix the bacon to the filet. Grind the black pepper onto a plate, and add in the desired amount of salt. Place the filet on the pepper, turning over to coat both sides.

Grill filets outside over hot coals or a gas grill to the desired degree of doneness.

Serves 4

Spaghetti with Chipotle Pecan Pesto

Pesto:
3 dried chipotle chilies
1 arbol chili
3 cloves garlic, peeled
1/2 cup olive oil
1/2 cup pecans
1/2 cup grated parmesan cheese
salt to taste

12 oz dry spaghetti, cooked, rinsed and cooled

In a small saucepan, boil chilies until tender, about 15 minutes. Remove chilies from water, and remove stems and seeds. Place chilies, garlic and oil in a food processor. Process into a fine paste. Add pecans and continue to process. Add parmesan cheese, and salt to taste. Pour over cooked spaghetti, and toss to coat the spaghetti well.

Makes 1 cup of pesto. Serves 4 - 6

Spiced Pears in Syrup

- 3 cups water
- 3 cups sugar
- 8 unripened pears, your favorite variety, very hard, peeled, cored, and quartered
- 1 fresh lime, washed
- 1" cube fresh ginger
- 6 cloves
- 1 stick cinnamon
- 2 cardamom pods

Boil water and sugar together, until sugar is dissolved. Squeeze in the juice of the lime, and add the used rind of lime to syrup. Add pears and spices, let simmer until pears are translucent, about 40 minutes.

Pears are now ready to be served, however, the flavors will be better blended if allowed to mellow in the refrigerator a few days. Process in water bath for canning, if desired.

Makes 2 quarts

Codorniz en Nogada

Codorniz en Nogada
(Quail in Pecan Sauce)

Arroz con Rajas
(Rice with Chile Strips)

Spinach Salad with Mustard Vinaigrette

Broiled Pineapple with Piloncillo

Serving quail is a great way to tell your guests how special their visit is to you. Farm raised quail are becoming increasingly available in our markets. However, if you can't find quail, substitute Cornish game hens, estimating one per person.

The broiled pineapple is about the easiest dessert I know. Have everything ready, but assemble and broil the dish at the last minute, so the fruit won't be soggy.

Codorniz en Nogada
(Quail in Pecan Sauce)

1 cup flour
salt and pepper
3/4 cup oil for frying
4 farm raised quail or 8 wild quail

Sauce:
1/2 cup pecans
1/4 cup onion, chopped
1 tbsp. parsley, chopped
salt to taste
pinch cayenne pepper
1/2 tsp. grated lemon rind
1 cup half and half
1/4 cup sherry
2 cloves garlic

Heat oven to 350°. Toast pecans in a baking pan for 6 minutes in the oven. Set aside.

Mix flour, salt and pepper on a plate. Heat oil in a skillet. Dredge whole quail in the flour, and fry for about 5 minutes on each side, until golden brown. Place quail in a baking dish.

Combine sauce ingredients in a blender container. Puree well. Pour sauce over quail, and bake for 30 minutes.

Serves 2

Arroz con Rajas
(Rice with Chile Strips)

1 poblano chile
2 tbsp. oil
1/4 onion, chopped
1 cup white rice
2 cups water or chicken broth
1 clove garlic, minced
salt

Roast the poblano chile in a gas flame or under an oven broiler and peel (see Basics). Cut out stem and remove seeds. Cut chiles into long strips. Set aside.

In a skillet, heat the oil. Fry the onion for about 30 seconds, then add the raw white rice. Fry the rice and the onion until the rice is completely opaque. Add in the water or chicken broth, roasted chili strips, garlic, and salt. When the water comes to a full boil, cover the skillet with a tightly fitting lid. Lower the heat to barely simmering. Cook rice for 25 minutes. DO NOT LIFT LID!

Fluff rice before serving.

Serves 2 - 4

Spinach Salad with Mustard Vinaigrette

10oz fresh spinach, well washed

Dressing:
1/4 cup lemon juice
1 cup olive oil
3 cloves garlic, minced
salt
freshly cracked black pepper
Grated Parmesan cheese

In a pot of boiling water, add spinach. Cover, and cook for 5 minutes, until spinach is wilted. Drain water, and chill spinach in the refrigerator.

Whisk together dressing ingredients, except for Parmesan cheese. Chill until ready to use.

Divide spinach into 2 to 4 portions, and place on small individual side dishes. Pour equal amounts of dressing over each portion of spinach, and sprinkle about 2 teaspoons of Parmesan cheese over the top.

Serves 2 - 4

Broiled Pineapple with Piloncillo

1 fresh pineapple
8 oz piloncillo

Peel and core pineapple. Cut into rings.
Place pineapple in a baking dish.

With a meat tenderizing hammer, break
piloncillo into small bits. (Piloncillo may be soft
enough to break up with your hands.) Then
place piloncillo chunks in a food processor.
Grind until you have small grains. Sprinkle
piloncillo over the pineapple.

When ready to serve, place pineapple under
a heated oven broiler. Broil for 7-10 minutes,
until piloncillo is bubbling in places.
Serve immediately.

Serves 4

Index

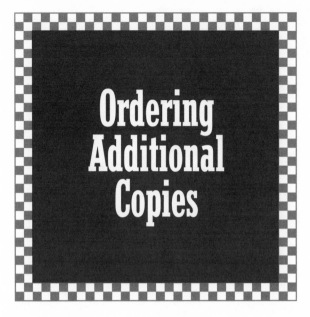

Ordering Additional Copies

To order additional copies of this cookbook, please fill out this form and send with check or money order to:

The Texas Provincial Kitchen

HCI Box 1

Linn, Texas 78563

Name and Address

Name _____

Address _____

City _____

State _____

Zip_____

Daytime Phone _____

Fax _____

Shipping Address (if different)

Address _____

City _____

State _____

Zip_____

Please send:

____ cookbooks @ $19.95 $_____

Add $2.00 Shipping per book   _____

Add 6 1/4% Sales Tax*   _____

TOTAL   ══════════════

Texas Residents Only